A Walk
around
Visalia

To Amanda
Keep walking!
George Pilling

by George Pilling

Sound Stories
Visalia, California

Cataloging in Publication data
Pilling, George, 1948–
A Walk around Visalia / George Pilling.
98p. 26cm.
Includes bibliographical references and index.
ISBN-10: 0-9665930-3-0 ISBN-13: 978-09665930-3-7 (paperback)
ISBN-10: 0-9665930-4-9 ISBN-13: 978-09665930-4-4 (hardcover)
1. Visalia (California). I. Title.
979.486 – dc22
Library of Congress Cataloging Control Number: 2011904102
©2011

Published by Sound Stories
1535 S. Grant St.
Visalia, California 93277
559-901-6676

For information visit www.georgepilling.com
First Printing, October 2011

Cover picture: Mill Creek in West Main Street Park

Cover design by Mark Ahlstrand

Book design by Charles King, www.ckmm.com

Dedication

*To two friends who
brought much joy
to my first years
in Visalia.*

Bard MacCallister (1918–2003), a folk
dancer and storyteller who dedicated his
life to the poor of Tulare County.

(Photo by David A. Warner)

Jim Doctor (1948–1993), a dancer
whose love of life was infectious
to all who knew him.

(Photo courtesy Vickie Stasch)

Acknowledgments

Writing a book like this is a community effort. I could not have done it without the help of many people.

Alan George prodded me to apply for a grant from the Tulare County Historical Society and then kept encouraging me to finish the book. Annie Mitchell was my taskmaster when I first wrote these articles. She was a tough but supportive critic. Norm Isbell of the College of Sequoias farm could identify trees over the phone. His help to this non-botanist was always kind. Mary Anne Terstegge, librarian in charge of the history room in the Tulare County Library until her death in 1999, always went out of her way to find the information I needed. John Lindt, founder of the *Valley Voice*, was the original inspiration for these articles, paying me $15 for each one I brought to him in 1993. Brian Kempf and Terry Ommen helped with information for revision of the articles for this book. Gary Lindquist provided the beautiful pictures of birds in chapter 12. City Engineer Eric Bons told me all I know about streets, sewers, and traffic lights in Visalia. Brian Motl gave me some burned out lights to take a picture of. My wife, Carol, walked with me and took notes. She also proofread the text before the pictures were added. My son-in-law Tom Chapppelear helped by reading the manuscript for a preliminary edit. Mark Ahlstrand of Madison Alley in Visalia created the cover, the maps, and helped greatly pulling it all together.

The staff and volunteers in the history room of the Tulare County Library helped immensely by finding facts and helping me to research picky details. Librarian Mike Drake found most of the historical pictures that are in this book.

I thank Charles King for his hard work in editing and formatting the text for publication. A few of the many other people who helped are mentioned in the text. The inaccuracies are mine – these people are experts. Thank you all!

Contents

Notes

Most of these articles were first printed in the *Valley Voice Newspaper* in 1993. This was before digital photography and few pictures accompanied the articles. Except for the historical photos and as noted in captions, all pictures in this book were taken by the author in 2008–2011. The original *Valley Voice* articles were updated and substantially revised at that time.

There are changes every time I look at these places. Plantings are changed, trees removed. Houses disappear and return in different forms. This is a snapshot in time.

After some debate, I decided to capitalize only the common names of specific species. As a result you will read "Coast Live Oak" and "oaks" "Screech Owl" and "owls."

Many friends have asked, and many more will ask, why I didn't include this or that beautiful walk in Visalia. I cheerfully donate the rights to the second volume to anyone willing to undertake it. Suggested walks: West Main Park to Pappas Park, Packwood Creek Trail, Santa Fe Trail, Blain Park and Green Oaks Drive, Royal Oaks Drive. There are many more.

—G.P.

Walk One

Jefferson Park to Paradise Avenue

Begin at Jefferson Park on Watson Street at Myrtle Avenue **❶**. Go south on Watson across Tulare and continue down to Paradise Avenue. Turn right on Paradise and stroll west to Conyer Street. There you will turn north (right) and continue to Mt. Whitney High School, then on to Myrtle Avenue. Turning east on Myrtle brings you back to Jefferson Park.

Jefferson Park

Jefferson School was built on this site in 1917 – a beautiful brick building with six classrooms. In the fashion of the day, it had white columns at the main entrance and a cupola over the middle. The cupola held the school bell.

The Field Act, passed by the California State Legislature after the 6.3 magnitude Long Beach earthquake of 1933, and later acts of the legislature, made unreinforced masonry public buildings obsolete. Jefferson School was closed in 1951.

Annie Mitchell, who taught sixth grade at Jefferson School 1933–35, watched her old school being destroyed. Workmen with sledges and tractors had no effect on the walls; a crane with a large wrecking ball had to be brought in to knock them down. The cupola was rescued and now rests in the back yard of

Laurelwood, the brick house at the corner of Giddings and Laurel.

Cupola of Jefferson School

H. E. Dye House

Watson Street is named for Wiley Watson. In the 1870s he used water from Mill Creek to water his peach orchard. He built an acequia (Spanish for aquifer) to move the water, one of many early irrigation constructions. Watson lived a few blocks northeast, nearer the town, with his family; the land around here was owned by a rancher, H. E. Dye. The Dye home, a Queen Anne style cottage built about 1900, still stands on the corner of Kaweah and Watson. It looks large and imposing on the outside, but inside it has small rooms with high ceilings. Recent owners have installed stamped tin and other touches.

Head south on Watson Street to continue the walk. At the corner of Laurel and Watson there is a rare thing in this part of Visalia – a vacant lot. Long ago there was a vineyard in this area and after that people planted walnuts. Remnants of the walnut trees remain in this lot and throughout the area are some tall trees that supply the jays and crows with food. Other walnut trees like these are only stumps that keep sprouting no matter how often they are cut down.

Across the street along the Mt. Whitney High School fence are planted Red-tip Photinia bushes. They were planted in 1991, replacing poisonous oleanders. Photinias are beautiful, especially in the spring, when new reddish growth appears. Take a close look at this hedge. It's fun to find the volunteer plants growing inside it. The Photinias were removed in 2011 and replaced with Jasmine, which will cover the fence.

Photinias

Just before Tulare Avenue there is a huge Italian Cypress in the Mt. Whitney yard. These trees are native to southern Europe, and in the U.S. are often planted in cemeteries and in small yards. It looks out of place here in the open without any graves around, but birds love the dense foliage for hiding their nests. At one time it was probably in the yard of a home. Another marker for a home site is the two palm trees that are here by the gate in the fence. Palms often flanked pathways to front doors or a driveway.

The traffic light at Tulare and Watson ❷ was installed in 2002. Lights are put in on streets that the city would like people to use as cross town arterials. Most of the lights are timed with each other, making traffic able to move faster.

A large Kumquat Tree shades the southwest corner yard here. The spring flowers of this tree fill the air with fragrance and the fruit is delicious.

Continue south on Watson Street and cross over Evans ditch, one of the many small canals in this part of town. Wouldn't this ditch – cleaned up and nicely planted – make a nice walking path through town? As it is, it is an eyesore.

Note the large Deodar Cedars along this part of Watson Street with their drooping blue-green branches and cones that stand straight up. Mature cones fall apart rather than fall off, dropping their seeds and litter under the tree. Deodars are native true cedars of the Himalayas.

Apricot trees are also native to that part of the earth; several are planted in this part of town. The apricot tree's dramatic shapes and dark bark are pleasingly intriguing. The early white or pink blossoms and the delicious fruit are added bonuses.

Paradise Oak

The Paradise Oak in January

A right on Paradise takes you to the Paradise Oak ❸. This 200-plus year old tree has withstood many automobile bumpers and is still in excellent shape. Its wide-spreading branches are home to many birds – winter is a good time to see how many nests you can count. Thank Visalian Alan George for his efforts in saving Valley Oaks whenever you see a landmark tree like this one.

Across Paradise is the old Seven-Up bottling plant, which is now a poorly maintained warehouse with junk scattered all over the yard. Recently, several apartments have been added to the front part of the old building. What a great place this would be for a small city park! The ditch could be opened and a few picnic tables installed. The result would get rid of the eyesore of the old plant and reduce commercial traffic in this residential area.

The hump in the road is caused by a branch canal that goes underneath. In the 1960s, this hump was even more pronounced and reportedly was a favorite place for young hot-rodders to "get air" when out for a joy ride. Bruce McDermott, former Visalia Police Chief, related that when he was a rookie, he chased one of these kids down Paradise Avenue. The civilian went over the hump with no damage, but the police cruiser came down so hard it blew all four tires. The young hot-rodder came back to make sure Bruce was OK before he went on his way – without a ticket.

The front yard of 608 W. Paradise in summer

Walking west on Paradise, note the nice group of California Coast Redwoods on the north side at Johnson. Their soft foliage with the cones at the tips, woodsy odor and resistance to disease make them pretty yard trees. They require much water though and may overwhelm a small yard quickly. It is nice to see a yard that is beautifully planted without any grass. Also note the small bare trees near the house. Two are Japanese maples, and the larger tree to the east is a deciduous magnolia, commonly called Saucer Magnolia or Tulip Tree. Their large tulip shaped fuchsia flowers will bloom at the end of February before the leaves come out.

Old and New

Grant Street was named for Robert Grant, who owned a bakery on Main Street in 1872. The house at the north end of this street, across from the tennis courts of Mt. Whitney High, was built in about 1890. At that time it was out in the country, about a mile from businesses downtown. The property was owned by Mr. O'Connell, and may have had a small vineyard or orchard which covered this area and was watered by Evans Ditch, which had already been established. This area was developed in the 1950s. Grant Street is only four blocks long but encompasses history – O'Connell's house at the north end is noted for its age; the one at the south end has solar panels on it to capture free electricity.

The home at 1535 S. Grant ❹ also shows how fast Valley Oaks grow. The Valley Oak in the front was planted in 1994. The ones on the Paradise street side of the house were planted in 1998. The two to the west, though, were planted in the roots of a tree that was removed; the difference in soil may be keeping them smaller than the one closer to the corner. Another oak was planted in the drought tolerant, lawn-free yard along Paradise in 2009.

Spring view of drought tolerant plants

Walking on to Conyer Street and turning north, you will see a small Valley Oak on the west side of the street that has more "oak apples" per branch than seems possible. These growths result from insects – oak gall wasps – which carve holes in the branches to lay eggs. The branch responds by creating a nest for the larvae. In addition to these most visible galls, there are several other varieties on this tree each caused by a different insect that depends on oak trees to reproduce. The galls do not harm the tree.

Across the street are two nicely cared for walnut trees which clearly show the native Black Walnut stump that the "English" Walnut is grafted on. The bark of these two varieties is so different that it is hard to imagine them grafting together. Native California walnuts, such as the Hinds Walnut, were used for the rootstock because they are resistant to soil borne diseases. (Nowadays a hybrid rootstock is used.) Black Walnut nuts are hard to crack and have small meats compared to the English Walnut – therefore the marriage by grafting is performed.

Just north of Howard Street on the left side ❺ is a large Ginkgo tree flanked by Coast Redwoods. The unique, fan-shaped leaves of the Ginkgo make a golden carpet under the tree when they fall. The Ginkgo is a gymnosperm, as are conifers and grasses – if you look at the leaves you will notice that the veins do not branch out like on most tree leaves, but go straight to the end of the leaf from the base. Ginkgoes are dioecious,

meaning that male and female trees are separate. Usually only male trees are planted because female trees produce copious quantities of smelly fruits that no one would want around.

Another landmark Valley Oak is growing here just before Tulare Avenue, dwarfing the house that it seems to be part of.

This kind of juxtaposition is what makes tree ordinances difficult in cities – people and property sometimes get hurt by falling trees. At the same time, all of Visalia's better neighborhoods contain many large oak trees. People fight the Visalia oak tree ordinance sometimes, and the city compromises when it "needs" to widen streets or make parking lots, but in general it works well.

Crossing Tulare Avenue again, you can walk through the nice little park formed under the pines, magnolias and oaks at the corner of the Mt. Whitney campus. Few students appreciate the mature trees around their campus, but we all benefit from their beauty and shade.

As you walk up the sidewalk past the front of the school, you will be under a row of Modesto Ash trees ❻. The first Modesto Ash was found growing in a park in Modesto with some Velvet Ash trees that had been planted there. Velvet Ash trees are native to the high deserts of the southwestern U.S., where they grow along washes. The found tree was probably a sport, or chance genetic mutation, and was named after the city where it was discovered. Modesto Ash grows more quickly than its native brother and gets larger, so it makes a better yard tree. However, many of the trees in Visalia are infected with various fungal diseases, which are exacerbated by over watering. Mistletoe often takes advantage of the weakness.

You may see some pecans on the pavement in front of the high school. These come from a tree across the street and are mostly dropped by Scrub Jays and crows who have found that the road and sidewalk make pretty good nutcrackers. Woodpeckers pick up the nuts the other birds lose and hide them in holes they make in trees and wooden poles. If you watch for a while you are likely to see Acorn Woodpeckers and Northern Flickers flying back and forth across the street.

Ginkgo leaf

Mount Whitney High

The school now named Mt. Whitney High School was opened in 1950 as Visalia Senior High School, serving eleventh and twelfth grades. Redwood High School took grades 7 through 10. It was not until 1957 that both schools had all four grades and Mt. Whitney High was renamed after the highest point in Tulare County.

Past the main entrance, swerve in toward the school to look at the Cork Oaks. These attractive trees, with their leaves that are dark green above and lighter below, are the commercial cork tree native to the Mediterranean region and Portugal. There, cork farmers use special axes to remove the outer bark of mature trees. The cork grows back and it can be harvested again in eight to ten years.

Head back to Conyer and north to the next street, Myrtle Avenue. On Myrtle, turn east toward the mountains. In the yard on the northeast corner is a large and nicely shaped Camphor tree ❼. Named for the odor of camphor in the crushed leaves, this evergreen is a native of China and Japan. The black bark and twisting, spreading limbs contrast with the dark green leaves to make the tree delightful all year around, although many complain about the almost constant leaf drop.

A Valley Oak at 808 W. Myrtle was the cause of quite a bit of controversy. The owner noticed that it was sick in the early 1980s. In 1991 a large limb fell off and grazed the roof of the house next door. The tree owner called a local tree service, which charged him a good amount to remove all potentially hazardous limbs. The tree service neglected to get a permit to do the work, so the city got into the act. Both the tree service and the owner of the tree were fined $500. The case wound up in court, but the fine held. The butchered tree did not survive and was ultimately removed.

California Bungalows

Myrtle Street was named during the building boom of the late 1910s, when the first three large subdivisions were erected in this area. Visalia Home Builder's tracts number 1, 2, and 3 were started before 1920, and now comprise the largest intact collection of California bungalows in California, according to Annie Mitchell, the late Tulare County historian. These homes were available in several sizes and styles, but all are essentially the same on the inside. (Anyone familiar with the bungalow floor plan would have no trouble finding the bathroom.) The owners, taking a clue from their street name, have planted Crape Myrtle trees along the sidewalk. The pink, red, and white blossoms are showy all spring and summer.

As you near Jefferson Park, you will note the eternal struggle between California Sycamores and sidewalks. The sycamores always win but, they have their own problems. Severe fungus infections make them lose their leaves early, before autumn. Birds love to tear apart the button-like seedpods, and the results – along with the strips of bark that fall – make a mess.

In 2008 a Screech Owl took up residence and nested in one of these sycamores on the north side of Myrtle. The owners of the house had to put up with not only the strange noises these

Cork bark

owls are famous for, but also the birdwatchers who flocked on their sidewalk at night, hoping for a glimpse of the owl.

At the southwest corner of Myrtle and Watson is Annie Mitchell's former home. I was lucky enough to visit her there many times while writing the original versions of these columns in 1993. She was a hard taskmaster who berated me when I got the local history wrong, but forgave me because at least I tried. I can imagine that she was one of those teachers that you always remember. She died in 2000, at age 92.

Years ago, you would have heard strange noises coming from around the houses north of the park. These were the plaintive love cries of Jefferson the Peacock, who flew in to the area sometime around 1985 but neglected to bring a mate. If you spotted him in the spring he was in full feather and raised his tail for you if approached. Jefferson loved to watch softball; his screams coming suddenly out of the oaks caused many a missed fly ball. Jefferson disappeared from the park in about 2003. Maybe he flew off to find true love.

A short stroll around the park will complete your two-mile walk. Jefferson Park is much used by the neighborhood and the city; you will rarely be alone there. Soccer teams use it for practice, there are softball games there all summer, and often a basketball or volleyball game is in progress. Families picnic under the oaks in right field, and it is a favorite meeting place of Mt. Whitney students before and after school. Recent improvements by the city of Visalia have added a sidewalk and a new playground complete with a climbing wall.

Walk Two

Memorial Park, Green Acres

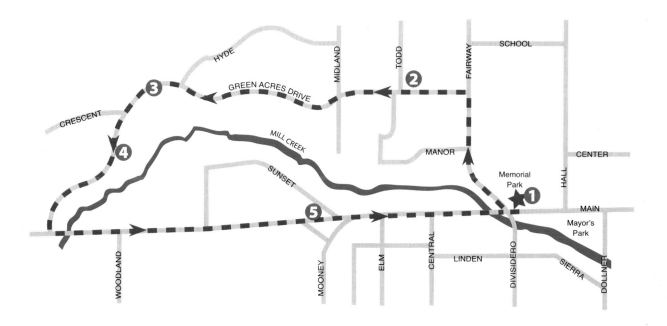

This walk goes through a neighborhood of large homes along Mill Creek.

Memorial Park

Park your car in Memorial Park – there are a few spaces off Main Street just west of Hall. The one acre of land for this park was donated to the city in memory of Charles D. Martin by the Martin family who are ranchers near Redbanks (between Ivanhoe and Woodlake).

Memorial Park ❶ contains several memorials worth noting. The cenotaph, a monument to people who are buried elsewhere, was dedicated in 1929. On each side of this obelisk is a plaque honoring Visalia's dead in the four wars of the twentieth century. Nearby is the Ralph S. Moore commemorative plaque and garden, and the plantings around the cenotaph are all Moore roses. The brick wall and arbor was erected in 2004. Ralph Moore, who died at 102 years of age in 2010, patented many varieties of roses and sold them from his nursery in east Visalia.

Cenotaph

The next thing you will notice is the trulli, the small building in the center of the park. The Byzantine design of this landmark was brought to Italy from the Imperial palace in Constantinople. In the heel of Italy's boot these ornate structures are traditional small houses. The people who live near Putignano, Italy, still use trulli as country hideaways – or even as homes. The story is that dwellings were taxed on their roofs – so the people made roofs that they could easily take apart when the revenuers were coming.

This trulli was built by hand in the 1980s as a reminder of the mother country for the many Visalians whose roots trace back to Putignano, Visalia's sister city. In Putignano, there is a bar named Bar Visalia. Maybe we should send them a California bungalow.

Memorial Park is nicely planted with a hedge of Laurustinus (*Viburnum tinus*) along the north side, whose clusters of white flowers bloom in February.

The deep purple berries attract many birds and the dense foliage gives them safety, so these bushes are usually alive with warblers, finches, juncos, and sparrows. There are also many spiders living here; their webs are beautiful on a dewy February morning.

The trees in the park are small Valley Oaks and Golden Rain trees (*Koelreuteria*) with their clusters of three sided seed pods at the end of their branches. There are many of these trees around Visalia about this size because a city arborist in the 1980s liked them. On the west end of the park you will notice a nicely shaped Valley Oak with the typical long spidery branches that sometimes hang all the way to the ground.

Go out of the park and carefully cross Fairway to walk north along Mill Creek. In season, Mill Creek rushes through here, full of extra water from Kaweah Lake and runoff from city streets and fields to the east. You quickly enter the serenity of the Green Acres neighborhood, with large houses and big trees to match. These oft-pruned trees contrast with the ones along Mill Creek which are generally wild and interesting, full of snags and nature. Come here in the early morning and listen to the many owls – Screech, Barn, and Great Horned are common, or observe the hawks that hunt here every day. I have seen Red Tailed, Red-shouldered, and Sparrow Hawks. A few years ago a huge flock of Swainson's Hawks settled in these oak trees for a week or two on their way north.

Green Acres Drive

Silk Oak trees are often planted in yards, like the ones across from the end of Green Acres Drive. These Australian trees are not true oaks, but have dense evergreen foliage and interesting compound leaves. This leaf configuration is unlike any native tree. They grow quickly and provide much shade, but Silk Oaks have some messy habits – they drop leaves and seeds year round, and drop large branches when the wind or a whim strikes them.

Turn west on Green Acres Drive and stroll along at the edge of the roadway. Willows are rare as yard trees in Visalia because of their need for water, but there is a good sized Weeping Willow in front of the house at 1914 Green Acres Drive ❷.

Weeping Willows are native to China – they are featured in many Chinese Paintings – but have been planted all over the United States, especially near lakes and streams.

Two Redwoods

Across the street notice a pair of redwoods. The one in front, with many short flat needles, is a Coast Redwood (*Sequoia sempervirens*), the species that grows the tallest of any tree on earth. The one behind, with scale-like leaves that barely stick out from the branchlets, is a Giant Sequoia (*Sequoiadendron giganteum*), the species that includes the General Sherman Tree and is native to our mountains at 6000–8000 ft. elevation.

Giant Sequoia

Coast Redwood

In 1993 there was a house at 2115 Green Acres. It was torn down around 1996 and now it is an empty lot with some nice Valley Oaks in back. On the eastern edge, two large Coast Live Oaks stand out. These evergreen oaks, native to the California Coast Range, are often planted here for their fast growing beauty. They are similar to the Interior Live Oak of the Sierra foothills but are considered more shapely, with their wide-spreading growth. On the west side of the front of this lot is a clump of Carob trees. The females of this Mediterranean native produce the long seed pods that can be ground up for a chocolate substitute. This tree's interesting growth pattern, with many sprouting trunks from the base and some long low branches, plus the fact that it is quite drought tolerant, make it a good choice for Visalia yards with sufficient room.

Privet berries hang over the yard of this Spanish style house

At the corner of Midland Street, and in many yards all over Visalia, there is a large, glossy Privet full of black berries that the birds love. Cedar Waxwings sometimes come in large flocks, settling in these trees and cleaning them of berries. Finches, sparrows, and juncos are also attracted. Bushes and trees that hold their berries through the winter are an excellent source of food for songbirds.

Farther down and across the street notice the bush that is covered with clusters of fragrant pinkish white bell shaped blossoms. This is a Strawberry Tree (*Arbutus unedo*) – one of the prettiest and most practical of ornamental trees in Visalia. It is a native of dry Mediterranean regions, requires little water and is resistant to fungus disease.

Along the north side of the street is a small grove of oranges amply protected by a hedge of Mock-orange (*Pittosporum tobira*). This shrub's circular leaf pattern and blossoms that smell like oranges make it a favorite for planting in the valley.

Coast Live Oaks

Varied Architectural Styles

On the left at the Valley Oak in the middle of the road ❸ is a colonial style home like one you might see in Massachusetts. Across from it is a true "modern" California house, long and low, with a palm tree out front.

This palm is in the group that is commonly referred to as "Mexican Fan Palm." The palm family is a huge group of trees with more than 2,600 species. They have been on earth since the age of the dinosaurs, and fossils have been found even in Greenland. Palms are different from most other trees in that they are monocots, as are grasses. The petals on their flowers are in multiples of three, their leaves have parallel veins and they do not add growth in annual rings. Palms grow all over the world in warm places. In the United States, there are about 10 species of palm native to Florida, and one native to California. The coconut palm is one of the most widely-distributed trees in the world because the nuts can survive long sea voyages, but it is not often planted as an ornamental because of the danger of getting hit by a falling coconut.

Around the corner on Green Acres Drive, on the left, is a nice big Valley Oak in front of a three-story house. In fact, if you peek through the hedges, you will see a few big oaks in their glory, dominating an expanse of lawn ❹. Our Valley Oak is a stately tree.

When you get to Main, cross carefully to walk east under the row of oaks. There are no sidewalks on either side, so this is the best choice. Note how the city is protecting the oaks on the north side, building the curbs around them. Also take a look at the rose bushes planted around the courthouse. The Tulare County Master Gardeners, a group of volunteers trained by University Cooperative Extension agricultural scientists in all matters about plants, maintain these roses and give hands-on classes on correct pruning techniques.

Cross back again at the corner of Main and Mooney to a unique memorial ❺. The plaque at the base of the tree commemorates the centennial of Sequoia National Park in 1990.

This Giant Sequoia was planted here then, and had grown to three feet high in 1993. In 2010 it is about twenty feet tall. If it should live another 3,000 years it would be 30 feet in diameter, but Sequoias rarely live more than 60 years in the valley. This one already seems to be suffering from die-back disease, *Botryosphaeria dothidea*, or another problem.

The cenotaph that is now in Memorial Park used to be near here. It was moved when Main Street was re-aligned in 1982.

Walk back to Memorial Park quickly to avoid exposing yourself to traffic for too long. Cross Mill Creek. Mayor's Park, on the south side of Main Street, is the subject of Walk Four.

Walk Three

Downtown

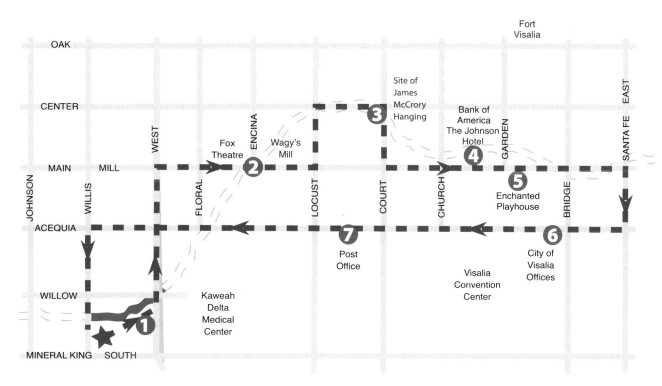

This month's walk is through the most beautiful downtown in the San Joaquin Valley, roughly following the course of Mill Creek, which wanders through central Visalia mostly underground. The creek was named for the three mills it powered in the late 1800s, one to cut lumber from mountain trees and the others to grind the grain produced by homesteaders.

Start in the middle of the Kaweah Delta Hospital complex, or campus as they call it, at the corner of Mineral King and West Street. For a few years, about 1995–2005, Kaweah Park, 7/10 acre of land, was here. In a compromise with the hospital, the park became a three-story office building. Mill Creek is still open just north of the building, though.

The Mill Creek Conduit

In 1912 citizens of Visalia passed a bond to build a concrete conduit to carry Mill Creek under the city. Before that, most of the creek within city limits was carried in a rotting plank flume. Garbage and loose vegetation made it stink, in addition to its being an eyesore and inconvenient to navigate around. The new conduit had (and still has) concrete walls eight inches thick and five feet high, a top slab 12 inches thick spanning nearly 15 feet, and was 2,725 feet long. It was started in early August and completed in November 1912. The total cost was $55,536, as bid. Built to carry a flood of 650 cubic feet per second, it held most floods before 1955, the flood that led to the building of Terminus Dam. Most of the conduit is still intact through downtown. A movement in Visalia to release parts of Mill Creek from its hidden travels has yet to go far.

The first, and only, part of the creek to be uncovered is the short section that wanders through the hospital courtyard ❶. The part behind the new office building, west of West Street, was never covered. For many years, students at Visalia High School (now Redwood) would push rafts up Mill Creek from where it flowed past the back of the tennis courts, into the conduit, and all the way to the mill race at East Street (now Santa Fe.) Then they could ride the flume back down to school, water level permitting.

In the late 1800s the city was bounded by four streets, called North, South, East, and West. Only West Street retains its name now. South Street was renamed Mineral King and North Street became Murray Avenue. We will follow Mill Creek upstream, walking on pavement above the creek from one end of historical Visalia to the other.

Crossing to the east side of West Street you can see that the creek banks have been planted with flowering pear trees over a succulent ground cover. Succulents are plants that store water in their fleshy leaves, which makes them able to withstand drought and also makes them fire resistant.

Also in this area are several Liquidambars or Sweetgum trees. Liquidambars are native to the southeast United States where their fall colors paint the southern Appalachian Mountains. Although popular as yard trees here, they have some problems: the fruits are hard, spiny balls that fall all year and are a pain to step on with bare feet. Their roots are close to the surface and can be hit by lawn mowers. Branches that start out parallel to the ground can break off when the outer foliage gets too heavy. Plus, Liquidambar's shape is erratic both in winter and in summer, with long branches making the trees look lumpy and lopsided. These are high prices to pay for a few weeks of autumn color. If you buy a tree, make sure to buy it in the fall and see the color of the leaves. The fall color varies from tree to tree and you could get a dud that just turns brown. A fruitless variety has been developed but is not widely available.

Kaweah Delta

As you stroll into the beautiful courtyard of the hospital (on a spur of Willow Street), you can see a short part of Mill Creek and the end of the conduit. The concrete rubble at the edges, probably left to protect from erosion, is part of the original conduit built in 1912. Daffodils on the banks add splashes of color in

A view of the Mill Creek conduit from
Kaweah Delta Hospital courtyard

Pagoda-like structure
in Kaweah Delta Courtyard

February and March, and an almost perfect ornamental pear tree graces the south side of the creek near the back entrance to the hospital. This tree has branches that reach out and up to make a dense wide crown. The white flowers are a treat in the early spring, followed by bright green leaves that turn red in the fall. The small, hard fruit is not messy and is enjoyed by birds.

With recent hospital remodeling, this courtyard has changed quite a bit, but it still is a great spot to enjoy a quiet lunch and many hospital employees take advantage of it. A more secluded spot can be found if you walk along the creek by the brick building. Tall Ailanthus trees (which are also known as the "Tree of Heaven") shade little two-bench patios that cantilever over the creek. Ailanthus are fast growing trees that sprout suckers freely from surface roots. They do well in cities, having a high tolerance for pollution, but they can also take over any outdoor area quickly if left alone. This is the species celebrated in "A Tree Grows in Brooklyn."

Mill Creek disappears here and will be underground for the rest of our walk. It heads diagonally past the front of the Fox Theatre, but we will have to walk in zigzags to follow on the streets above. Walk through the parking lot of Checkers hamburger restaurant, then up Floral to Main, which was originally called Mill Street. The brickwork along the curbs and the plantings that are so well kept emphasize Visalia's downtown beauty. Four different species of trees add variety to this corner – two pines, a Bradford Pear, a Star Magnolia, and a Camphor Tree. Underneath are *Nandina*, Box, Azalea and *Pittosporum* bushes with pansies planted for color.

Flowering Pear Tree on Main Street in March

Fox Theatre

The Fox Theatre ❷ was built in the early 1930s. It had stars on the ceiling, elephants painted on the exposed beams in the lobby, and a clock that you could hear ticking loudly when in the women's bathroom. On its large stage appeared the Vienna Boys Choir, the Robert Shaw Choral, operas, and the Miss Tulare County pageant, for which a runway was extended into the seats from the stage.

In 1997 a non-profit group formed to purchase and restore it to its former glory. The owners, finding a good way to ease themselves of a huge liability, generously gave the theater to the Friends of the Fox, and reconstruction soon began. Huge amounts of volunteer labor and over $500,000 has not been wasted. The theater is now glorious, with original wall paintings painstakingly restored and the clock in working condition for the first time in over 25 years. There is still

Abe's Pet Store was for years near this corner. It was a ritual for many families to stop and look at the puppies in the window on walks downtown. Now we can look in the windows of fancy shops and restaurants and often wave to our friends dining inside, but it's not quite the same.

Head east on Main to Encina Street. Encina means "evergreen oak" in Spanish. Originally this street was named for another tree, the Cottonwood. Undoubtedly there were some large native Fremont Cottonwoods near Wagy's Mill, which was in this block. After progress put the creek underground and cut down the cottonwoods, the name was changed to the more poetic, and by then more accurate, Encina.

The restored Fox Theatre

Elephants walk on the beams

Murderer Lynched

Walk north on Locus to Center, then east to Court. Mill Creek goes directly under this intersection ❸. It was here, in 1872, that James G. McCrory was hung for murder by having one end of a rope tied to his neck and the other end to the railing of the bridge on Court Street. He was thrown over the side to hang above Mill Creek. Mr. McCrory was not, however, tried or convicted for murder. Local citizens, convinced of his guilt (there wasn't any doubt), took the law into their own hands, dragged him out of jail, and lynched him.

Mill Creek goes diagonally under Court Street back to the alley behind Togni Branch stationers. It then goes right under the Bank of America Building. In the 1800s and early 1900s there were several Chinese laundries along Mill Creek. They used the water to wash clothes and bedding from the hotels. Chinese people were accepted as members of the community, although many laws prevented them from gaining full rights of citizenship.

much more to be done, but the events that now can be staged here bring life to downtown.

Follow Main to Locust noticing the lively downtown activity. New businesses are springing up all over. The restaurants are excellent and well patronized. All along Main Street the Urban Tree Foundation and masses of volunteers have planted trees. This nonprofit, started by Visalian Brian Kempf, is dedicated to preserving the urban forest. Tree plantings, held regularly, are a fun way for families to contribute to the beauty of Visalia.

Main Street in 1863 –
the earliest known picture of Visalia

The same view of Main Street in 2011

The Johnson Hotel

The finest hotel in Visalia – and perhaps the whole central valley – was the Johnson Hotel ❹. Constructed in 1916 at the NE corner of Main and Church Streets (where the Bank of America is now), it catered to the many travelers up and down the valley from Stockton and the bay area to the farms of Tulare County and on to Los Angeles. Fire destroyed the Johnson Hotel in May 1968 and it was torn down that summer.

During the flood of December 1955 the hotel management had all the canned goods from the basement brought up into the lobby so they would not be ruined by the flood waters. When the waters receded enough for the food to be moved back downstairs, though, another problem had arisen. A log had become lodged in the Mill Creek conduit somewhere under the alley behind the hotel. The blockage prevented any water from getting past it, so the water, under huge pressure from the weight of the water upstream, started coming out in strange places. The hotel basement was still flooded. Manhole covers were lifted into the air as the water poured out. Spurts came through cracks in the floor of the DeSoto dealership at Santa Fe and Main. Water threatened to come up everywhere.

The city had to find the blockage, so

out came the jackhammers to pound through twelve inches of aged reinforced concrete covered by the asphalt of the alley. The first hole was dry – it was downstream from the blockage. Moving east, they walled the alley with sandbags and dug a second hole about where the engineers thought the blockage was. They hit water, which gushed up, ran along the alley and fell back in the first hole. So far, so good. But they were too far upstream of the blockage to remove it.

They brought in a crane with a clamshell digger to dig more holes and found the blockage. But when one log was pulled out, the plug moved ten feet down the creek and stuck again. A final hole succeeded in releasing the water, and the December flood was declared officially over on January 30. Rick McClun tells this story humorously and well in a pamphlet in the history room of the library.

Carob trees encircle the Bank of America building. These attractive trees with dense, dark green, glossy foliage are drought tolerant once established. They are native to the Eastern Mediterranean, where they are known as "St. John's Bread." St. John must have liked chocolate because the seedpods of carob trees are the source of the chocolate substitute found in health food stores. Female trees grow fruit, which dry to dark brown, flat, hard pods over a foot long. To eat one, you break the pods open and discard the seeds then chew on or grind up the pod. It is rich in sugar and does taste a little like chocolate.

Turn back to Main Street and walk east to the Main Street Theatre ❺. In a strange twist of fate, another nonprofit remodeled this theater at the same time that the Fox Theatre was being fixed up. Susan Sluka Gutierrez, founder of The Enchanted Playhouse Theatre Company, saw the chance of a lifetime and convinced her board to lease the old run-down movie theater in 1996.

They spent thousands of volunteer hours and more than $150,000 in donations to change it into a community live theater space. It is the home of a superb company, which produces four family-oriented plays a year. In 2003 the bay area owners decided to sell it. The city, seeing its value as a community theater, used eminent domain to try to take it over. A lawsuit ensued involving a church that claimed to be willing to purchase it, which was finally settled with a compromise that the church and the Enchanted Playhouse would share the theater. Soon after that the church dropped out, so the Enchanted Playhouse has full use of the theater for now.

Fort Visalia

Look north to the site of the original Fort Visalia, built in 1860 on the corner of what is now Oak and Garden Streets. It was established ostensibly to protect settlers from Indian raids, but it also made clear California's support for the union in the years before the civil war. Many Visalians were from the south and sympathized with the confederate cause. The soldiers in the fort kept the peace as much as possible. The lumber store that occupied the site is out of business and there is some rumbling about the city purchasing this block for a historic park. Sounds like a great idea!

Bridge Street was named for the first bridge across Mill Creek, built in the early 1850s. Fifteen men arrived and settled along the Kaweah twelve miles east of here in 1850. After an altercation with the natives only five remained, and they moved west into the fertile floodplain. By 1852 there was a permanent settlement. The U.S. census shows a population of 548 in 1860.

Santa Fe Street was originally East Street, the city's end. As you walk south on it you pass the site of the Matthews Brothers mill, the first mill on the creek. Matthews Brothers set up a millrace heading south from the creek through their mill and then west along "Sakie" Street (later formalized to Acequia, meaning waterway in Spanish). We will follow this route back.

In the parking lot of the city offices on Bridge Street ❻ is an interesting tree – a Laurel Leaf Snail Seed (*Cocculus laurifolius*). This native of the Himalayas is wider than high and has interesting leaves with three distinct veins that run from the base to the tip. Birds enjoy the black berries.

The small trees in the planters on the north side of the convention center are Bayley Acacias which show clusters of bright yellow flowers in February and March. The leaves are tiny and dense with an interesting gray-green color. These trees will be magnificent when they grow to full size.

Post Office

The Visalia Post Office ❼ opened in 1937. It was built as a part of the WPA – Roosevelt's plan to get the country working again – and is an excellent example of the architecture of its time. Note the beautiful detailing in the

Post office detail

brickwork and ironwork on the outside, then walk into the lobby to see the art deco style ironwork over the service windows and other architectural decoration.

Southern Magnolias and Giant Sequoias were planted on each side soon after the building was erected. The Sequoia on the east side died in 2006, probably of die-back blight, *Botryosphaeria dothidea*, a blight that attacks Sequoias in the valley. It was replaced with a small Coast Redwood, which was about five feet high in 2009. In 2010 this new tree died. The post office manager told me "I think that spot is haunted. We have decided not to replace the tree again."

Visalia Post Office

This 1.2 mile walk continues along Acequia Avenue back to Floral where the Matthews Brothers' waterway rejoined Mill Creek. The new hospital buildings have made many changes along this block, including the new parking garage on the north side of Acequia.

New Kaweah-Delta Hospital wing

As you walk back to your car, notice the flat area north of Mill Creek. There are several Valley Oaks, but one of the trees is different. It is a Hackberry, a member of the Elm family native to the eastern United States. These trees have nice, spreading branches, tolerate heat and pollution, are resistant to oak root fungus and cast a lot of shade. But they are prone to getting white flies, which causes them to leak messy sap on anything below them.

On the banks of the creek are some Fremont Cottonwoods, named after the famous explorer of the Colorado River. The ancestors of these trees grew along Mill Creek for centuries before anyone thought of putting a city here.

You can learn much more of the interesting history of Visalia by going on a walk with Terry Ommen or other members of the Tulare County Historical Society. For starters, check in the history room in the library and explore the history museum in Mooney Grove Park. There are lots of fun details to know and more to discover.

Walk Four

Mayor's Park, Redwood High

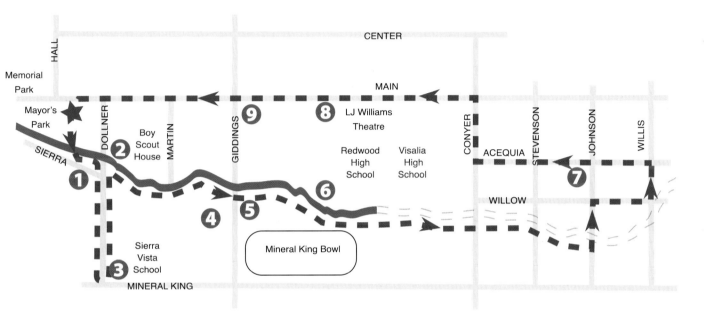

Mayor's Park straddles Mill Creek on Main Street near Divisadero. The creek separates the cultivated side – mowed grass dotted with Valley Oaks and Deodars – from the wild side, south of Mill Creek, overgrown with Periwinkle (*Vinca*), blackberries, sweet peas and Virginia Creeper all in a wild profusion. Mulberries, oaks (Valley and Coast Live) and other plants grow untended.

This walk starts on Sierra Drive and goes through Redwood High School and back along Main Street to the cultivated side of this nice one acre park.

The houses across Sierra Drive are interesting. The southwest style house with the second floor veranda and the carved beams that hold it up is rare in this area. Other houses are Tudor Revival style with high peaked roofs that flare out to curve over the entryways.

Walking upstream (east) along Mill Creek, there is a forest of riparian growth ❶. The native trees are the Valley Oaks, Fremont Cottonwoods, and California Sycamores, all of which do well near streams. One sycamore here is probably the largest in the area – it may be over 100 years old. Large Pyracantha bushes fill in the middle levels. The ground cover is mostly Periwinkles (*Vinca*) native to Europe but extremely invasive wherever they are planted. Blackberries grow well in wet areas, and there are many here. They are native to parts of California, plus there is a Himalayan variety that grows wild here with the California one.

There is a story that a Johnny Appleseed imitator came through Tulare County in the 1800s with blackberry cuttings, planting them in every wet spot. He thought he was doing a good thing, but ranchers and others have been fighting the brambles ever since. The blackberries grown commercially are varietals and crosses: Boysenberries and Olallieberries are some familiar crosses with other similar berries. The wild berries here are delicious if you can find them before the birds do

As you come to the end of Sierra Drive you will see a nice spot of irises next to a fence on the right. These wonderful flowers bloom year after year without any help, reproducing prodigiously. They tolerate long periods without water and different colors flower in turn nearly every month of the year. All they need is to be thinned every few years – and this results in many gifts to make your friends happy.

On the left at Dollner is a pretty little almond tree growing up in the middle of the fence, its black bark contrasting

A jungle at the Dollner Street bridge over Mill Creek

beautifully with the white boards. Over the bridge hangs a wisteria vine growing up in a Black Walnut. The walnut's trunk is completely wrapped in English Ivy and both the ivy and the wisteria bloom high into the branches.

The Log Cabin

Cross Dollner into the parking lot of Sierra Vista School. Until 2000 there was a log cabin here that was made as a Boy Scout house in the late 1940s ❷. Now volunteers have transformed this area into a park and walk. The cabin was moved to the Tulare County Museum in Mooney Grove Park. Moving the cabin brought up interesting issues in land ownership. No one claimed the land the cabin was on – the city said it belonged to the school district, who thought it belonged to the boy scouts, who never used the cabin – so no one kept it clean or trimmed the plants. The result was both a mess and an interesting assortment of trees – some of which have become very large specimens. A huge juniper grows near where the chimney of the cabin was. Tulip trees grow at the other end of the cabin site. A thick-trunked poplar with much sucker growth from the base gets its water from the creek. Black Locusts, mulberries, and willows abound. A Loquat grows in the shade of the larger trees. The school district and the city, with volunteer labor, have cleaned this up and are now maintaining the property.

A little about some of these trees: Poplars, which include Cottonwoods and Quaking Aspens, have thin oval leaf stems that allow the leaves to shake in light breezes. This action may help the tree by deflecting the force of a wind away from the brittle branches, the side-to-side motion of the leaves absorbing shock. The shaking motion may also expose more leaf surface, including the undersides of leaves, to sunlight, thus increasing photosynthesis. Poplar woods are used in such products as Hopi Kachina Dolls (traditionally made from the root of the Fremont Cottonwood) and excelsior evaporative cooler pads, as well as being a secondary wood in furniture construction. Native Fremont Cottonwoods grow in Visalia and are noted in some of these walks, but this poplar is a variety from the eastern U.S.

Tulip Tree blossom

Tulip Trees, also known as Tulip Poplars, will grow to be 80 foot tall giants with branches that spread to 40 feet wide. They are named for the two inch tulip shaped blossoms produced on mature trees each spring. The leaves, with two shallow indentations that make three blunt points, turn bright yellow in the autumn. The popular name is very confusing because this tree is not a poplar at all, but is part of the magnolia family. Also, the Saucer Magnolia is commonly called Tulip Tree, but looks nothing like this. The scientific name of this tree is *Liriodendron tulipifer*.

Black Locusts, with their compound leaves that have up to 19 little round leaflets on each leaf, are also native to eastern states. Black Locust is prized for the hard, rot-resistant wood and the beautiful white or pink blossoms. It is a drought resistant tree that was brought to California with gold seekers in the 1850s. The wood is used for durable fence posts.

This juniper is a little of a mystery. It is a huge specimen tree, but none of the experts I have asked could tell me what species it is. Juniper berries (the fleshy seed cones) flavor gin, and the rot-resistant wood also makes good fence posts.

Loquats, natives of Eastern China, produce sweet orange fruits with big seeds. They have the unusual trait of flowering in November and producing their fruit in early spring. Some people believe that the fruit has a calming effect if eaten in quantity.

Sierra Vista School

Sierra Vista School, now an annex of Redwood High School that is used for language and math classes, was built in 1939 as an elementary school and was used for kindergarten through sixth grade until 1966. It is a beautiful building with decorations typical of the 1930s.

Sierra Vista School

The Rotary Theater was the auditorium of Sierra Vista School. Now it is used by various school and community groups.

A bond passed in 2004 allowed Visalia Unified to completely remodel the Sierra Vista campus. The Art Deco elements were kept and enhanced while the building was brought to modern lighting, access, and earthquake codes.

The two small trees on each side of the steps up to Sierra Vista School are a Bottlebrush and a twisted juniper. The Bottlebrush is native to Australia, and gets its name from the long flower clusters with red stamens that stick out like bristles.

Take a short detour past the Rotary Theater to take a quick look at the mural on the south side of the building ❸. Sponsored by Read for Life, the Tulare County non-profit that encourages parents to read to their children and gives thousands of books away each year, this mural was painted in 2000 by artist Varian Mace.

Walk back to the creek and start along the path ❹, heading east to Redwood High School. The chain link fence along the creek is an eyesore. There is work underway to make a nice walking path along the stream here. As you walk along the fence, you will see several large eucalyptus and ailanthus trees interspersed with the native and other non-native trees. Scrub Jays, crows, Brewer's Blackbirds, warblers, sparrows, finches, woodpeckers and many others are active here. It would make a fine outdoor biology laboratory.

This walk is crowded at least seven times a week day as students travel back and forth. They are only given six minutes between classes and some students make the trek four times a day from the main campus. The constant foot traffic and many cars on Giddings were an accident waiting to happen, with several close calls occurring weekly. Parents of Redwood students formed a committee to raise money to build the crossing bridge you see here now; it was finished in 1995.

When the gates are open, Mill Creek can be followed most of the way through Redwood High. Go past the water tower and all the trails that students use to try to sneak into Giant Chevrolet Bowl, formerly Sunkist Bowl, but still best known by its pre-advertising name, Mineral King Bowl.

Mill Creek near Sierra Vista School

The water tower ❺ is part of California Water Service's network. It was taken apart and moved from just south of Noble Avenue to this spot when Highway 198 was built. It is 95 feet high, not including the police and fire radio antennas on the top. This height would give approximately 45 pounds of pressure at the ground. The tank holds 300,000 gallons. When system pressures were low it was used to regulate pressure, but with a new pumping system this is not a problem. Now water is pumped into it during off-peak hours to be used when demand is great.

Note the cattails in the creek here, which indicate easily attainable water and sunlight. Cattails and other bulrushes were traditionally called tules here in the Western U.S. and the first explorers of the valley encountered miles of them around Tulare Lake, which was named for them. They are a source of food for people and animals and a source of fiber that can be used to make a silk-like cloth. They are the favorite home of Redwing Blackbirds, which build nests between the stems about a foot above the water.

As you walk through the handball courts, you will notice the plantings getting more cultivated. That is because you are approaching the Redwood Agriculture Department on the south side of the creek.

Leave Mill Creek and wander into the Redwood courtyard ❻, planted with at least 10 different species of trees including Aleppo and Canary Island pines (with the 12 inch needles), Ginkgoes, Carob Trees, Mulberries, evergreen and deciduous magnolias, flowering pears and, of course, Coast Redwoods. The planters contain India Hawthorn (*Rhaphiolepis Indica*) with pretty pink flowers and large dark berries.

Leave the courtyard, cross Conyer Street and go back to walk along the south side of Mill Creek. This is another part of our city stream that has been recently (2005–6) landscaped with volunteer help. Until then, it grew wild, with lots of trash next to an open field.

Crossing Stevenson to walk behind the police and fire departments, you will see several species of tree from the Mediterranean region of Europe planted along the creek here. Raywood Ash, with leaves that have seven to eleven thin oval, serrated edge leaflets, is grown for its purple red color

WELCOME TO
MILL CREEK TRAIL

THIS TRAIL WAS DEVELOPED TO PROVIDE A NATURAL SETTING FOR THE COMMUNITY TO ENJOY AND WAS MADE POSSIBLE THROUGH A PARTNERSHIP BETWEEN VISALIA UNIFIED SCHOOL DISTRICT, CITY OF VISALIA, SERVICES EDUCATION AND EMPLOYMENT PROGRAM, SEQUOIA RIVERLANDS TRUST AND THE URBAN TREE FOUNDATION.

THIS SECTION OF THE TRAIL IS VUSD PROPERTY. THE DISTRICT RESERVES THE RIGHT TO CLOSE THE TRAIL WITHOUT NOTICE.

MILL CREEK TRAIL

TRAILS OF VISALIA

in the fall. Holly Oaks are named for the evergreen leaves which are often sharply pointed along the edges. Cork Oaks develop the thick bark that is harvested for profit in some parts of the world after they are 15 or more years old.

Mill Creek disappears temporarily at Johnson and goes under Rosa's Restaurant, but it reappears in the middle of the medical office building at Noble and Willis. A stout Valley Oak at the corner of Noble and Willis dwarfs nice clumps of Japanese White birches.

Look to the north along Willis. When these articles first were written, the prospect was bleak – open sidewalks with no trees. The Urban Tree Foundation, started by Brian Kempf, has planted hundreds of trees along Visalia's streets. You can see the results here. The trees you see looking north are only a few years old (planted around 2003-4), but they have already made a huge difference in the ambiance of Visalia's streets. These are Forest Green Oaks, a cultivar of the Italian or Hungarian Oak (*Quercus Frainetto*) which is native to the Mediterranean region as are many plants that do well in our climate.

City Hall

Turn west on Acequia, heading back toward Redwood High. City Hall ❼ is beautifully planted with shapely, yellow flowering Willow Pittisporum shrubs in the planters along Johnson and Azaleas underneath. Next to the entrance to City Hall is a large and beautiful Xylosma. These versatile plants can be grown as shrubs or trees, hedge, or even ground cover. They require moderate water and tolerate heat well. The leaves are shed in April while the new ones are coming out.

At the west end of city hall is a wide spreading Southern Live Oak, native to the southeastern U.S. This is the tree that you see hung all over with Spanish Moss in *Gone With the Wind*. Spanish Moss is an epiphyte that needs to get water from the air; it will not grow here.

Cross Conyer Street into the redwood forest and walk across the grass to main. This "forest" consists mostly of Coast Redwoods, but look closely and you will see one Giant Sequoia in with them. The large Deodar Cedars along Main were planted in 1912.

Redwood High School

In 1911 Visalia's new high school opened here. On a Friday night two months later it burned to the ground. By the next Monday Lincoln Primary school-classes were placed in homes, businesses, and anywhere else they would fit. High school classes returned to the Lincoln School on the Oval, where they were before. The new high school was rebuilt and opened in 1912.

From 1927 to 1941 this campus housed Visalia Junior College as well as Visalia Union High School. The college moved out to the country on Mooney Boulevard in 1949. The last class to graduate from Visalia Union High was in 1950. In September of that year, Visalia Senior High opened three blocks south on Conyer Street and this Main Street campus became the junior high for seventh through ninth grades.

In 1954 half the tenth grade students stayed and named this campus Redwood High School, while the senior class all remained at the newly named Mt. Whitney High. Green Acres Middle School opened that year to take care of the 7th and 8th grade students. Divisadero Middle School opened in 1956.

The library at Redwood is named for Tulare County's historian Annie Mitchell, who died in 2000 at age 91.

Montgomery Auditorium

L.J. Williams was the principal of Visalia High School and Visalia Junior College from 1928 to 1947. Williams became the first president of the newly renamed College of the Sequoias in 1949.

Although this building ❽ is commonly referred to as the L.J. Williams Theater, it is only the newer part that changed it from an auditorium to a theater in the 1970s that is named after Williams. The building is officially the Montgomery Auditorium, named for DeWitt Montgomery, superintendent of Visalia Schools from 1919 to 1946, and L.J. Williams's boss.

Art Deco Corinthian columns line the front and sides of an otherwise Mission Revival style building, blending styles that were popular in 1932. The 1972 additions are in a different style but blend in surprisingly well. The side wings made the theater safe and accessible for theater goers and the additions to the back of the stage made it possible to produce real plays here. Before the backstage fix, people remember watching the backdrop curtain ripple as actors moved to positions for their next entrance. The only alternative was a cold run around the back of the building.

Across Main, notice the Craftsman bungalow style houses with brick columns on the porches. Some of these columns are made of clinker brick. Clinkers originally were the failures in the kiln that were overheated, but later they were made for their decorative effect. These bricks were popular through the early 1900s.

The home at 1300 W. Main Street was built in 1915 by Benjamin Dudley, the man who discovered oil in the Lost Hills west of Bakersfield. His father, Moses, was a Tulare County pioneer cattleman and rancher near Elderwood – his ranch is still in operation, with his great-granddaughter now in charge. Ben discovered oil, then returned to Visalia and became a land developer, building homes along Main Street west of Giddings in what was called the Parkside Tract. The house was purchased by the Wesleyan Church, but later returned to private hands. It is now an office building.

The tree on the northwest corner of Giddings and Main is an Italian Cypress. These trees are native to southern Europe and north Africa so they also do well in our climate. Landscape architects use their columnar shape like an exclamation point to emphasize a special feature of a building. They do not grow quickly; this one is very old, and it looks odd because the lower branches have been trimmed off. Italian Cypresses were popular in the early 1900s as yard

Lone Oak Park

Continue to Giddings Street, past the softball field. At the corner of Main and Giddings, in the middle of the intersection ❾, was the smallest official park in California. Lone Oak Park was eight feet nine inches by six feet seven inches. It contained one large Valley Oak tree, which the city protected from 1900 when Main was paved until 1936 when the worry about liability convinced a majority of the city council that its removal was necessary. By then the tree was deeply scarred at bumper height, festooned with pieces of chrome and glass, painted white and covered with ineffective reflectors.

1300 West Main Street

may have been brought to Tulare County by early settlers interested in starting silkworm farming here.

Both colors of berries are delicious. If they happen to be in fruit when you pass by, pick some to eat for dessert.

trees, and this huge one probably was planted then.

The land for Mayor's Park was donated by C. J. Giddings when he subdivided his property here. It was dedicated in August 1916. You can eat your lunch at the picnic table then stroll across the bridge over Mill Creek. As you enter the bridge notice the tree growing in and around the concrete bank of the creek. It is a fruited or female Mulberry. This one, and the other volunteers like it along the creek, has profuse quantities of berries from May to July, which are favored by birds as well as by smart people. The red or black-fruited variety is most common around here, but there are also trees with fruit that is white when ripe. The white fruited one, native to the orient, is the host tree for silkworm caterpillars and

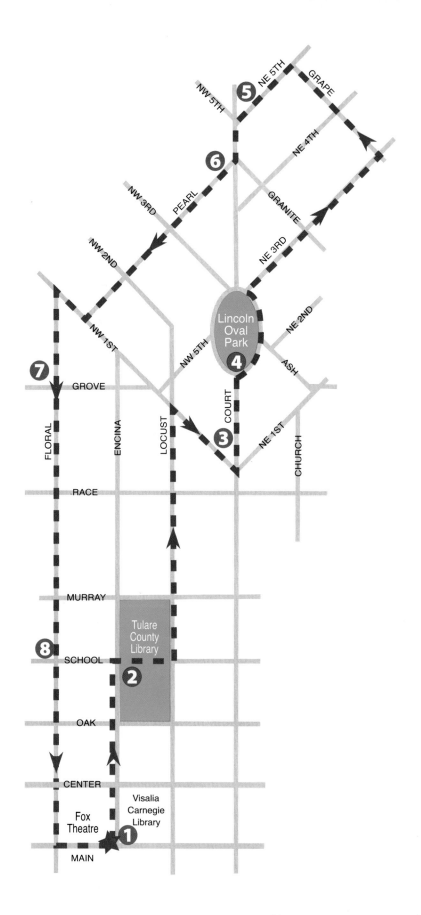

NE 5TH

GRAPE

NW 5TH

5

NE 4TH

6

NW 3RD

PEARL

GRANITE

NW 2ND

NE 3RD

NW 1ST

Lincoln
Oval
Park

4

NE 2ND

GROVE

7

NW 5TH

ASH

FLORAL

ENCINA

LOCUST

COURT

3

NE 1ST

CHURCH

RACE

MURRAY

Tulare
County
Library

SCHOOL

8

2

OAK

CENTER

Fox
Theatre

Visalia
Carnegie
Library

1

MAIN

Walk Five

The Library and the Oval

This walk starts at the site of the former Carnegie Library in Visalia on Main and Encina, goes to the present library, then north on Court, around the oval, and back to Main via Encina Street, with a few detours.

Visalia passed an ordinance to establish a free library in 1903. Before that, there was a private "reading room" at the Good Templar's Hall as early as 1873. The first public reading room in Visalia was

Visalia Free Library, Visalia, Calif.

started by the Women's Christian Temperance Union in 1893. In 1902 Carnegie library building funds were applied for, and 33 books were received from the University of California Extension Traveling Library Service.

Andrew Carnegie, the Pittsburgh steel magnate and extraordinary philanthropist, gave more than $56 million to build libraries in English-speaking countries. One thousand seven hundred libraries were built in the United States before 1917. The Carnegie Foundation still gives money for libraries and literacy.

The Visalia Carnegie library stood at the corner of Cottonwood Street (now Encina) and Mill Street (now Main,) east of where the Fox Theatre was later built ❶. It opened on May 31, 1904. Miss Grace

Hurlbut of Nebraska was hired to be Visalia's first librarian. In 1906 Miss Hurlbut left her job to get married and her assistant, Mary McEwen, succeeded her at a salary of $40 per month. She retired when the new $36,000 PWA funded library was built in 1936.

The 1936 building was, until recently, known as the "old library." From 1977–2000 it was variously used for storage and as an annex to the Senior Center across the street, but was closed in about 2000 because of an invasion of mold. It is a beautiful building. The entrance and tile roof are in the Spanish Colonial style. The two original wings welcome the visitor into the octagonal center tower.

Before the 1936 library was built, this prime spot in the middle of Visalia ❷ was the site of Visalia's first school, the "Little White School," which opened in 1857. This was replaced in 1872 by a wood two-story school known as Visalia School, and was replaced again in 1890 with the Tipton-Lindsay School, a three-story brick building. Both of the last

schools had high belfries to call children to class.

The Tipton-Lindsay School had 14 classrooms on the bottom two floors and an assembly room on the third floor. High school classes were held in this hall until 1897, when Visalia High School opened on Lincoln Oval. In 1917 Tipton-Lindsay school was closed. By that time six other elementary schools had opened plus the new high school.

The city of Visalia purchased this block from the school district in 1917 as the site for a library, but it was not actually built until 1936. A children's wing was added to the old library in 1961, but by the 1970s Visalia had completely outgrown the old library. Increasing concern and regulations about earthquake safety also prohibited investing more in the beautiful building.

In 1975 the city and county together built the "new" library building, a simple large open space with room for a few offices and meeting rooms upstairs. It was completed in 1976 at a cost of $1.5 million. The county library moved over from the basement of the courthouse, and the city of Visalia gave up the small amount of property tax earmarked for the library to the county. It officially became the Visalia branch of the Tulare County Public Library.

Ceiling in the 1936 library, now part of new children's area

Library Moving Day

Moving a library is a huge job. Every book must be kept in order so that it can be put back in the right place. Merging libraries is even more complicated. There are many horror stories of professional movers putting all the books in one big pile for library staff to sort out later. Great planning by Art Stobbe, the city librarian who retired soon after the 1976 merger, enabled this move to go smoothly.

During the first two weeks of November (1976) both the city library and the county library (in the basement of the court house two blocks away on Court Street) were closed. Staff from both furiously moved and merged the two book collections. Everything had been planned, even to the amount of shelf space needed and where. Trucks full of books came from the county library while the city staff moved books out of their old library and into the new.

Every book was color coded with little dots that showed whether they were going to storage or the new shelves. You can still sometimes find a little red or yellow dot on older books. All the furniture, too, was color-coded to the room it was to be moved to and each staff person had designed a plan of how his or her space would be arranged.

Everything went smoothly, except that the elevator had not been inspected and so it could not be used. One desk was carried upstairs to the office; the rest of the furniture waited for that detail to be completed. Art Stobbe made many trips to Hagopian's (the Armenian deli that was on N. Willis Street) for food for the hardworking staff. Master alphabetizers merged the card catalogues over the next several months.

When Proposition 13 passed in 1978, the city was very glad that it had already given complete responsibility for the library to the county. The small amount of property tax dedicated to the library is not enough to maintain it – the county adds general fund money to support the library system. The city of Visalia is only responsible for the grounds, which it still owns.

In 2007 with much fundraising and support from the federal Library Services and Construction Act, Tulare County was able to bring the two buildings together. Both the 1935 and 1976 buildings were repaired and rebuilt. They were joined with a newly created circulation area. The older building is now the children's area while the 1976 building houses the adult collection. A popular section for teenagers is in the corner of the adult area. The new library was dedicated on October 28, 2008.

The new children's area
in the 1936 library building

Walk around to the east entrance of the library to find a pretty sculpture. Mrs. H.G. Eichmann gave this birdbath to the city of Visalia In 1941. It was sculpted by Carroll Barnes from an imported block of Carrera marble and weighs

700 pounds, not including the concrete base. Eichmann was the wife of local piano tuner and music teacher, Harry Eichmann. They were patrons of the arts and also loved birds. Barnes, the sculptor, was the world famous artist who lived in Three Rivers. His other work in Visalia is the College of the Sequoias Giant, created out of a redwood trunk.

American Elm near
new east entrance of the library

The Eichmann Birdbath

On the grounds near here is a fence around what looks like a well. It is actually a reverse well; it is used to pump storm water back underground for storage. Groundwater recharge is an important component of Visalia's water system. In the 1800s the water table was close enough to the surface that people could hand-dig wells here. Now the water is over 100 feet deep and sinking.

Library Park is planted with small Valley Oak trees, which the city is using to replace the old and rotting American Elms. One American Elm remains, on Locust Street. All others have succumbed to Dutch elm disease. Along the sides of the old library are Chinese Pistache trees which turn beautiful colors in the fall. Fern Pines (*Podocarpus gracilior*)

are planted along the walls of the new library, along with Heavenly Bamboo (*Nandina*).

For variety, a Liquidambar tree is planted in front of the old library and a Golden Rain tree (*Koelreuteria*) is planted in front of the entrance to the new library. Around the corner, along Locust Street, are some Honey Locust trees. The Honey Locust is native to the Eastern U.S. These trees are fast growing, pretty, and have strong wood that doesn't rot, but watch out for long, wicked thorns on branches. Other trees in this area are redbuds, Canary Island or Spanish Longleaf Pines, and sycamores.

Old Houses

Head North on Locust Street for a block, then cross over on Murray to Court Street.

Locust was one of the first streets in Visalia to have homes on it. The House of Volunteers, at 417 N. Locust, is believed to be built on the site where Nathaniel Vise pitched his tent. The present Colonial Revival house was built in 1921 with extensive remodeling after a tree fell on the home in the 1930s.

The Queen Anne style house at 509 N. Locust was built in 1901 for hardware merchant R. F. Cross. The high foundation was needed to prevent floodwaters from entering the parlor. Across the street, the home at 518 N. Locust is the only remaining one of eight Italianate houses built on this block in the 1880s.

533 N. Locust shows a transition from formal Victorian to the more casual bungalow style. The rounded porch and the accents around the windows are Victorian, while the windows and lower ceilings reflect the bungalow influence. This house was built by C. J. Berry, manager of the Johnson Hotel, in 1910.

The book *Visalia's Heritage* is an excellent source of information about these homes. The library also has brochures which will lead you on several historical walking tours around the old homes of Visalia.

If you have time, stroll down the 500 block of Court Street, which also has some of the oldest homes in Visalia.

Rainbow Bakery

At NW First Street, turn right and make a detour through the Rainbow Bakery building ❸. It was built in the 1920s, using locally made brick. It was originally the Visalia Baking Company. J.A. Sutton owned the business, making bread and cakes under the brand names "Sally Anne," "Holsum," and "Rainbow." Baking continued into the 1970s, when the factory closed. Redevelopment funds rehabilitated the building into attractive office space in 1992.

Rainbow Bakery Building

The Oval

The wide decorated sidewalk along Court Street leads right to Lincoln Oval Park ❹. Lincoln Oval was part of one of the first additions to the original Visalia town site. This land was owned by Gideon Aughinbaugh, who received it in 1859 in trade from Tulare County for farmland that the county wanted to use for a public cemetery. The county wanted the cemetery moved outside city limits and Aughinbaugh owned the perfect spot on Goshen Avenue (where it still is today.) Aughinbaugh sold the land to the city. He later moved north and founded the city of Alameda.

The large Deodar Cedar near the south end of the park serves as Visalia's Christmas tree. American Elms are planted around the edges of the park, all of them showing signs of Dutch elm disease. Some Shamel Ash trees are also in poor shape, but the Valley Oaks are doing well and the large Coast Redwoods give good shade.

In 1897 Visalia's first high school was built here. When Visalia High School (now Redwood High) opened in 1911, this school became Lincoln Elementary School. The first kindergartens – a new idea in the 1910s – were at Lincoln and at Washington schools. In 1922 Lincoln School was declared unsafe and was torn down.

Stop for a bite to eat at a unique spot – Ofelia's. Ofelia has been serving tacos through her window since the 1970s. After eating, stroll part way around the oval to NE Third Street. Note the nicely cared for old homes at 109 and 117. An Incense Cedar in the front yard of 117 gives constant greenery plus a nice odor.

The stores here show the varied ethnicity of this area. Brothers Oriental Market serves the Laotian immigrants, while La Fiesta market deals in Mexican specialties. This area around the oval has always been racially mixed. One block over (on NE Fourth Street) was the first school in Visalia for African-Americans, known as the "Visalia Colored School."

Opened in 1873, it served the African-American and Mexican-American communities plus any Native Americans in the area. The teacher, Mr. Daniel Scott, was paid by the Visalia Unified School District. The school building was little more than a shack, with a pen and garden area outside for students to learn farming. The bathrooms were also outside.

The "Visalia Colored School" ca. 1875

Some nearby districts sent their "Negro" children to this school in Visalia, but if the distance was over five miles in those days few children of any color went to school. Many small school districts in Tulare County allowed children of color to attend the same school as white children, but Visalia did not.

In 1888 Arthur Wysinger, a 16-year-old, applied for admission to Visalia Public High School. He had graduated from the highest class available in the "colored" school. He was denied admittance on the basis of his race – he was African-American. The Wysingers brought suit and lost in the local courts. But in January of 1890 the Supreme Court of California reversed the lower courts. The case was the first school segregation lawsuit in California and one of the first in the United States. The Wysinger family had moved to Oakland by the time it was decided.

Turn left on Grape Street and notice the large red-barked eucalyptus tree at the edge of a vacant lot. These trees withstand drought and abuse yet remain strong. Note the dense rounded crown casting much needed shade. Although the story is that the first eucalyptus were brought here by mistake – Aussies would not give away any good timber varieties – these hardy trees are successful here.

Head back to Court Street on NE Fifth Street. Here the yards are beautifully cared for, with many large trees – magnolias, oaks, pines, ash, eucalyptus, acacia, and others. There is not much fancy here, just people proudly caring for their own property.

Specialty Beverages operated three bottling lines in the run-down building on the corner of Court and NW Fifth Street until 1991 ❺. The factory operations moved out to the winery near Orosi on Highway 63 then, but this eyesore remains.

Wittman Village

Jog south on Court to Pearl, past the Wittman Village Center and Village Park ❻. This community center is run by a non-profit corporation that was established with the help from the city of Visalia. Sports coaching, classes, and a study hall are provided. Breakfast and lunch are provided for school-age children who are on vacation.

Where the diagonal streets meet the North-South East-West grid, there are some interesting triangles. These make pleasant little parks that often contain large trees and interesting flowers. They are cared for by the city and by the people in the neighborhoods around them.

Triangle Park

Mixed housing uses in this area make the single family homes less desirable, yet most of the homes are proudly cared for. On the corner of NW Second Street, the owner has tied together two mulberries to make a green arch over the front walkway.

Pearl dead-ends into NE First Street under a grove of sycamores. Jog right to Floral and head south.

Thick buttresses and wide eave boards distinguish the Harry J. Hays house at 829 N. Floral. This shingle-sided Craftsman bungalow was built about 1910 for Hays, who was a director of the Mt. Whitney Power Company.

Before the corner of Floral and Grove ❼, you will pass under one of the largest Chinaberry Trees in Visalia. The large violet flower clusters in May are followed by copious quantities of hard yellow berries. The berries can be poisonous if enough are eaten, but birds like them.

First Cadillac in Town

Looking to your left, the structure at 208 West Grove is the Spalding Carriage House ❼. It was built as a garage for the Spalding House, which is the large colonial revival home at 631 N. Encina. William Spalding owned a lumber company and evidently did very well. He had one of the first automobiles in town – a

Reo Roadster. His wife had the first electric car in Visalia, a Baker. In 1907 Mr. Spalding bought a new Cadillac, which he protected by remodeling this garage to accept automobiles.

At the corner of Floral and Race, the Queen Anne cottage with a corner porch covered by a flared roof was built by C.J. Giddings in 1905. Giddings was a banker and the treasurer of Visalia. The George Deppler Smith house is across the street – a large shingled Craftsman bungalow from 1910.

The Silver Maples along Floral here cast a nice shade and seem to do well in the valley even though they are native to the Eastern U.S. where they are considered little better than trash trees. Silver Maples grow fast and are well shaped, but the branches break easily and the leaves turn a dull brown in the fall (unlike the bright reds of the Sugar Maple, which does not grow well here). The Silver Maple is named for the gray bark and silvery underside of the leaves.

Many of the old houses in this area are being turned into offices. The Colonial Revival house at 403 N. Floral ❽ is now law offices; in 1902 it was built as a wedding gift for J.E. Combs and his wife, paid for by the bride's father, S.C. Brown. The clinker brick and the shingles show the influence of the new Craftsman style,

Tulare AND FRESNO **Record** EXAMINER.

VOLUME I.   VISALIA, CALIFORNIA: SATURDAY MORNING, JULY 9, 1859.   NUMBER 3.

while the symmetrical design and the details of the roof overhangs emphasize the Colonial style.

The *Times-Delta* Newspaper claims its 150th year in 2011, but that claim is a little arbitrary. The first paper published here was the weekly *Tulare County Record and Fresno Examiner*, in June 1859. The offices and press were in the basement of the county courthouse. After two months of publication, it was purchased by John Shannon, who was a Democrat and southern sympathizer. He changed the name of the paper to the *Weekly Delta*. In September 1860, William Gouvneur Morris started the *Visalia Sun*, which supported Republican causes and President Lincoln. In November of that year Morris and Shannon met in a duel over editorials. Morris shot and killed Shannon. He was acquitted on the grounds that Shannon was the instigator.

On his deathbed, Shannon asked his attorney, L. O. Sterns, to take over the *Weekly Delta*. Sterns soon sold it to two men who changed its policy to support the Union cause, and by the end of the year the *Delta* had absorbed the *Sun*.

Visalia was not a one-paper town for long. *The Equal Rights Expositor* started in September 1862. This weekly strongly supported secession and southern causes.

In March of 1863 Union troops from Fort Visalia entered the office and threw the presses into the street in protest of an anti-Lincoln editorial.

In 1865 another weekly started, the *Tulare Times*. This paper was also successful, but it was not until 1892, under the leadership of owner Ben Maddox, that it became a daily paper, delivered in the afternoon. On the same day, the *Delta* started publishing daily in the morning. On March 1, 1928 the two papers merged, creating the *Visalia Times-Delta*. In 1967 the press moved from the corner of Acequia and Court to this block with the offices fronting on West Street.

Turn left on School and return to the library. At the corner of Floral and School is an Eastlake style Victorian cottage built in 1896. The owners are repairing it to its former beauty. The spindle decoration on the porches and the curved brackets over the windows are hallmarks of this style.

Head back to Main Street where we started. There are lots of places near here to get a bite to eat after your 2.5 mile walk.

Washington School, built in 1908

Oleander flowers

Walk Six

Washington School

This month's walk will go through an old part of Visalia with many historic houses. Along with old houses are mature trees and shrubs, glorious in their summer foliage. We will start at Washington School, travel up Garden, down Church, back north on Court, wind around a little and return to the school's well-used playground.

The Washington School area has become somewhat run down over the past 50 years. As in many parts of the city, the school serves as the focal point and main meeting place for the community. Parents see each other when picking up their children or dropping them off and begin neighborly interactions. A community association formed in 2008 promises great changes for the area.

The original Washington School was built in 1908. It was the second elementary school in Visalia and the first on the south side of town. The building was a handsome two-story with three big Spanish-style arches over the entrance and two three-story towers. A tall flagpole stood exactly in front of this symmetrical structure. The 1908 building was torn down and replaced in 1950 with the buildings that you see.

Flowering magnolias outside the entrance add a bit of color to the drab architecture. In the playground are ash trees, deodars, and two large, untrimmed fruitless mulberries. Mulberries will grow well without being trimmed, and

will provide more shade than those that are cut back to stubs each year.

If your mulberries have been trimmed, however, you can't just suddenly decide to stop cutting them back in the fall. If you do, the weight of all the new growth

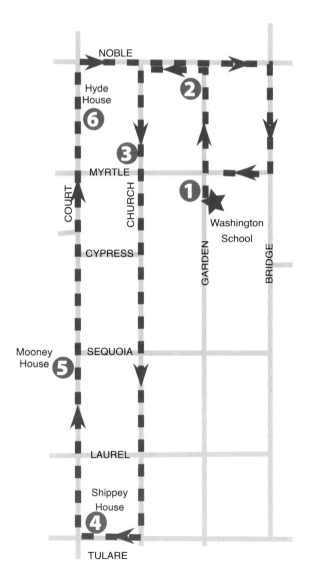

on weak limbs could break the tree. It is possible to restore mulberries to normal tree growth, but it takes a few years of trimming less and less each year until the branches are strong enough for the growth.

The house across from the school entrance, 513 S. Garden ❶, was built in 1906 by Billy Campbell. The house has mixed architectural styles with mostly Colonial Revival elements. The flared, complex roof is rare for this style of home. Billy was an auto mechanic and drove in the Fourth of July automobile races that were held in downtown Visalia. These races were sponsored by the American Automobile Association and drew crowds of up to 50,000 people to the area between 1911 and 1914. Since the population of Visalia was 5,000 in 1911, these must have been amazing events.

Walking north on Garden, you may notice a nice plum tree in the yard at 446. Plums were planted in Tulare County by early settlers, and became a crop after the 1870s when the railroads made it possible to transport the fruit to markets. Prunes, which are dried from a kind of plum, were very popular in the early part of the 20th century. Dried fruit is easier to transport and keep than fresh, of course. Plums are still the 10th highest grossing crop in Tulare County.

Across the street, 431 S. Garden is a California bungalow with the original wood shingle roof (it may soon be replaced as it is in poor shape.) Note that every sixth row of shingles is doubled. This was a purely ornamental custom which was done to emphasize the long, low horizontal lines of the bungalows. Wood shingles were sawn from blocks of cedar or redwood on special sawing

431 S. Garden St.

machines that were known as finger eaters – shingle-making was a dangerous job. More common on roofs today are cedar "shakes" which are split, not sawn. However, fire insurance requirements make it nearly impossible to replace a roof with any kind of wood now.

As you near Noble Ave., many of the old houses have become offices. One of these is the headquarters of the Sequoia Riverlands Trust ❷, a land trust that purchases and maintains ecologically important acreage throughout Tulare County. This organization started when it took over management of the Kaweah Oaks Preserve from the Nature Conservancy. Since then it has grown quickly as people who want to protect their special places donate and sell easements and land to them. The Trust has a strong educational program now, involving hundreds of people in events at their preserves around Tulare County.

Turn left (west) at Noble. The oleanders along the freeway are in full bloom in the summer. The ones across Noble are a unique coral color.

Church Street

Turning left again on Church, you can see the varied plantings that come when old and new parts of town are nearby. Large old California Sycamores show signs of the anthracnose fungus they are susceptible to. Liquidambars, Chinese Elms, and palm trees surround the new offices.

Church Street is named for the earliest churches in town, which were mostly north of here closer to the city center. The first church service held in Visalia was organized by the Methodist-Episcopal church in an open air spot near Fort Visalia in 1852. In 1857 this sect opened the first church building at 100 S. Church Street. Catholics were not far behind: the first Mass celebrated in Visalia was in 1861. In 1865 Gideon Aughinbaugh, owner of much of the land in north Visalia, gave a brick livery stable he owned to the Catholic Church. This served for a few years until a new church was built in 1869 on that lot at 500 N. Church, which is on the grounds of George McCann Catholic School now.

436 S. Church is one of only two Dutch Colonial Revival style houses in

437 S. Church St.

Visalia. It was built in 1908 and has a gambrel-roofed second story that overhangs the front porch. Across the street is a large two-story craftsman bungalow, built in 1910 (above). Elements of this style and the related shingle style are evident in the heavy knee braces supporting the eaves, the tall windows with divided panes above and the asymmetrical facade and porch column treatment.

The Steuben house, at 444 S. Church, is still occupied by the family of the original owner. The Steubens ran the Wells Fargo agency in town beginning in the 1870s. They built another house next door and joined the two homes with a substantial brick and iron fence. The row of large pecans in the front yard was planted about 1915.

449 S. Church ❸ was built in 1902 and, in addition to the predominant Queen Anne style, shows Colonial Revival styling in the double columns on the porch and Empire styling in the mansard roof above the bay window. It all makes for

449 S. Church St.

an interesting facade, which is about to be lost to view by the overgrowth of privet, pecan, mulberry, and eucalyptus.

Stop to smell the large, wildly grow-ing gardenia in front of 502 S. Church. Gardenias are na-tive to China, grow well here with some protection from summer sun and put out their fragrant

944 S. Court St.

blossoms from May through October. Even when not in flower, their glossy green leaves are beautiful to look at. Another Chinese import, the Weeping Willow, overhangs the front yard and the sidewalk.

727 S. Church has been stuccoed in a pattern to make it look like it is built of rock. Some of the higher "rocks" are separated by wood moldings that tie in with the window casings. The decoration makes this otherwise plain rectangular house more interesting.

Note the large beaver tail Prickly Pear in front of 809 S. Church. These thorny plants have large showy flowers of many colors (this one pale yellow) and edible fruit. The pads also can be scraped, cooked, and eaten – they make a great addition to scrambled eggs. In the wild, these plants supply safe homes for small rodents and birds. A large lo-quat tree stands behind it, next to the house. Loquats are edible fruits native to China.

Travel south on to Tulare Avenue and turn right. The next street is Court, where you will turn north again.

Curved Home

Just before the corner is a fruiting Black Mulberry tree with the best tasting mul-berries I have ever had. These are not bland like most mulberries, but each berry is as flavorful as a blackberry with that slight tartness that hits your tongue just before being overwhelmed by the natural sugar. Try them on your morning cereal for a treat! This wonderful tree is in the yard of 944 S. Court (the berries hang over onto public property and so are fair game ❹). This home was built in 1903 by a carpenter, Daniel Shippey, who evidently liked curves – the curved windows on the wrap-around porch are unique. His design skills were not lost on his son, Alvin B. Shippey, who, in addition to running a planing mill and lumberyard, designed and built many buildings in Visalia and Tulare County including the Palace Theatre in Lindsay. A. B. Shippey lived in the Eastlake style house around the corner at 910 S. Court.

Walking north on Court, you will find an empty lot at the corner of Laurel Street. This is owned by California Water

Service and was formerly a well site. In fact, there were four wells on this lot at various times in the past and that makes it difficult to drill another because of the danger of the property caving in and taking the well drilling rig with it. California Water Service is trying to find a site for a new well nearby but doesn't want to risk drilling here again.

The Mooney house is at 807 S. Court ❺. Now divided into six apartments, it was built in 1875 as the large home of Michael Mooney, the first mayor of Visalia. The Mooney family owned the land from Cypress Street to Tulare plus many acres of ranch land. As the Mooney children grew up, other homes were built along Court Street for them.

As you walk north, note first the Italian Cypress with its upright growth that completely hides the trunk from view. Half a block farther north, at 717, is an Incense Cedar (native to California) which has drooping branches that are open to see the trunk all the way to the top. The scale-like leaves look similar, but the growth habits of the trees are quite different. Also note the Catalpa tree, with the long bean pods hanging down in the fall and with showy white blossoms in early summer, and the small California Redbud, which will tolerate the shade of the Catalpa and cedar quite well. Catalpas are native to the eastern U.S., but the Redbud is a native of Tulare County, although it has been transplanted, like the cedar, from the foothills down here to the valley.

Across Court Street is the Church of Christ. Built in 1908 by a group of German Lutherans, it has been in

Church of Christ

continuous use since then. The simple lines are given a Gothic flavor by the high pitched roof built in three successively higher gables. The utilitarian double hung windows are capped with arched stained glass panes.

The multicolored paint jobs sported by some of the Victorian houses in California (such as 614 S. Court) are not the original paint scheme on these houses, but they are fun and certainly colorful. Older generations tended to let the decorative elements speak for themselves more subtly; in our fast, drive-by times we may need the color to catch our attention.

The Hyde house, at 500 S. Court ❻, was built for Richard Hyde in 1886 and is in beautiful shape thanks to caring owners. Hyde started the Bank of Visalia, where the Bank of the Sierras is now on Main Street. The first story brick, once stuccoed, is now exposed and the shingles on the upper story appear in many patterns from rounded "fish scales" to sawtooth to staggered. Half timbers top it off on the front gable and

The Hyde House

a Chippendale-style railing surrounds the porch and is echoed in the fence around the property. The entrance gate is overarched with joined Italian Cypresses. Cupid wrestling with a swan tops a birdbath. A pair of antique street lamps adds to the pleasing eclecticism. Hyde died in 1917, but his estate was not settled until 1936 when it was valued at $500,000 – in the middle of the depression!

Turn east on Noble and return to Bridge Street where you can look south to the former olive plant. Cute little homes, mostly small bungalows, are along Bridge. More and more of these beautiful homes are being fixed up. As you return to Washington School, note the curiously heavy braces on the porch of the bungalow across from the school on Bridge Street. The owner of this

house will not have to worry about the typical bungalow problem of a sagging porch roof.

You have just walked about 2 miles through an interesting neighborhood. Many homes are in need of repair, but the variety of old styles and mature plantings are pleasing.

Walk Seven

Cemetery

If you can ignore the folklore, cemeteries are excellent places to walk. They are wide open spaces with more trees than there are on golf courses and there are no little white balls to dodge. History is as alive as it gets in the cemetery, too. Each monument recalls the bare details of someone's life – preserving at least that much memory for the future.

The first Visalia Cemetery was at Locust and Race streets. It was established in 1854, but only five years later it was deemed too close to the rapidly growing city of Visalia and was moved to its present site. A land swap deal was made with Gideon Aughinbaugh, who owned most of the land around the present day Lincoln Oval. He traded five acres of farmland for the five acres in town on the condition that he move all the bodies already interred.

There is no record of how many caskets were moved, but the process took more than a year with relatives of the deceased contacted to select new burial sites and with moving headstones (most of them actually boards), foot stones, and even fences and other enclosures that were popular then.

The first recorded burial in the new cemetery was in September of 1860.

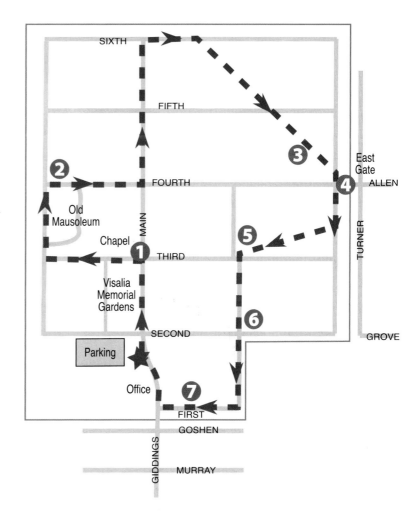

Since then, approximately 50,000 people have been buried here.

Giddings Street turns into the cemetery's Main Street after you enter the gates, past Goshen Avenue. There are parking spaces right next to the office inside the gate. Next to the office is the veteran's memorial, constructed in 2009–2010.

Head north up Main Street. The cemetery is arranged in sections with small

A view up the cemetery's Main Street

street signs marking the borders. The newer sections are easily picked out because there are no standing markers in these areas. This is for ease of mowing – the drivers of the mower have to have special training on obstacle courses before being allowed to mow the old sections.

Varied Trees

Several newly planted trees are along Main Street. A few small Tulip Trees (*Liriodendron*) and a Raywood Ash on your right (east) will soon shade this section. Farther up an English Hawthorn, now covered with berries, is a glory in the spring with showy pink or red flowers. A Liquidambar drops its prickly balls near the Visalia Memorial Gardens Mausoleum.

Two ginkgoes, with their fan-shaped leaves, are on both sides of the street

and behind the mausoleum are two pecans and a Camphor tree. The palms in front of and inside the mausoleum are Mediterranean Fan Palms.

Visalia Memorial Gardens is the new mausoleum. Constructed of marble in 1966, it was expanded in 1985. Both bodies and ashes are entombed here. A space for a body is called a crypt while the space for ashes is called a niche. Double or single crypts are available.

Many people purchase their crypts or plots in advance. As you walk through the cemetery, you will see many gravestones that do not have the dates of death on them yet, which means that the person mentioned on the stone is still alive. Although it would probably be cheaper to have the date of death filled in when the stone is purchased, most people pay a little more to keep it uncertain.

Tom Davis, who worked in the cemetery in 1993, told me about one couple

The new mausoleum

who came in to purchase a "pre-need" grave. They were both in their eighties and wanted a double grave so they could be interred on top of each other. The arrangements were made, but the next day the woman came back alone. She told him that she was changing her will. Tom allowed as how it was a good idea to put the new arrangements in writing

The firemen's memorial

so there would be no confusion among the heirs. The woman replied, "No, you don't understand. I want to change what we talked about yesterday. That man I was with is my fourth husband. I've out-lived three others before him. But I've decided that I want to be buried with husband number two – he was the best of all four."

The firemen's memorial, at the corner of Main and 2nd Street, was erected in 1948 as a monument to all the firemen of Visalia. Behind it is a big Italian Cypress that is not in good shape – either stressed by something in the soil or dying of

old age. It and some others nearby do not even look like the usually straight, thin, densely foliated, dark green Italian Cypress.

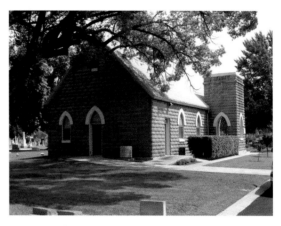

The Cemetery Chapel

The chapel was built in 1911 ❶. The project was funded by the city of Visalia and the Ladies Improvement Society, who had taken charge of the cemetery grounds in 1896. The Gothic Revival style is imitated in cast cement blocks intended to remind visitors of large cathedrals.

By 1981 the building had deteriorated to such a point that it was about to be removed when a "Save the Chapel" com-mittee was formed. This group raised enough money to refurbish the building, which was rededicated in 1986. Funerals and memorial services with up to 50 people can be held there. It is also avail-able for small weddings, but none have been held there in recent years.

Walk west down the Third Street to-ward the Old Mausoleum. Crape Myrtles and two small Giant Sequoias stand out-side the door. Although you have to have a relative buried inside to be allowed in, you can appreciate some of the beauty of this building from outside. Built in 1921, it sits low and solid with only a

little decoration on the face. Inside are marble doors, stained glass windows and some comfortable chairs. The border of the ceiling is painted in an Art Deco design. Only a few spots are empty and all of these are already reserved.

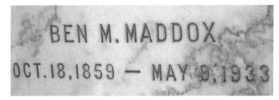

Ben Maddox's crypt

Behind the mausoleum is one of the county sections where people are buried at government expense. Most of the markers here are simple cast concrete. In the 1800s and early 1900s many people who were buried here were not even named. Entries in the cemetery records stating "A Mexican Woman" or "A Chinese Man" were common in the 1800s. Most of the white people were named, however.

The section just north of the mausoleum contains an area called "Baby Land" ❷. Here are smaller graves, mostly from the days when childhood death was common. Walk back to Main Street, passing under the wide spreading fruitless mulberry, which has been allowed to grow freely to reach its true glory.

Ash Trees

Walk north on Main in the shade of the ash trees. There are many varieties of ash all over the world and hundreds of hybrids and cultivars (plants selected for desirable characteristics) are available. They are fast growing trees with strong but flexible wood that is used to make baseball bats (the wooden kind.) As you head north, the graves are newer, but the plantings are beautiful all over the cemetery. In fact, plants are changed so

often here that this book must be considered one snapshot in time, and not portray present reality.

Section A, on the east side of Main, contains some graves from the 1800s. Most of the marble and granite obelisks you see date from the 1880s to 1910. A few are cast in the shape of tree trunks, denoting members of the Woodmen of the World and Women of Woodcraft societies. It is nice to see the simplest graves next to the grandest monuments.

At the corner of Main and Fourth, note two Chinese Pistache, a Chinese Elm and (down Fourth a ways) a large Catalpa. Catalpas are native to the Southeast United States but are very adaptable. They have large clusters of white flowers in the spring, which result in the long seed pods you can see hanging on the tree all summer. The huge leaves provide thick shade.

All Hallows

North of Fourth street you enter "All Hallows Cemetery," the section owned by the Catholic Church. This section was established soon after the cemetery was moved here in 1860 and was completely administered by the Catholic Church until the keeping of public records by public agencies became mandatory sometime in the 1920s. Other sections were purchased in the 1860s

by the Masonic and Odd Fellows lodges, Jewish, and Chinese groups.

There are more interesting trees along Main Street in this section. Some Honey Locusts, with compound leaves having many small leaflets are on the west side of the street. Further along is a persimmon tree. This one is the American Persimmon, native to the Southeast. The fruit, small and green in the summer, will turn bright orange and hang on the tree after the leaves have fallen, making an interesting Christmas tree. This type of persimmon is delicious and sweet when completely soft, but don't attempt to eat one before it is soft. A hard persimmon will pucker your whole insides.

Looking to your right (east), you will see two long rows of ash trees extending through All Hallows Cemetery. Walk along in their shade. The monuments are varied. Simple concrete markers lie next to elaborate sculptures that depict the progress of civilization – from rough granite to a Corinthian column all on one stone.

The George McCann tomb

Turn right before Sixth Street if the grass is dry and head across the grass to the larger monuments near the east edge. The largest of all is the resting place of George McCann ❸, for whom the school attached to St. Mary's church is named. Peering inside, you can see that his personal life was hard – most of the markers are for children and young adults.

In 1924 McCann's widow donated $24,000 to establish a nunnery and a school for the Catholic Church in Visalia. The school had four classrooms, taught by four nuns who lived in the convent with a fifth nun who cooked for them.

A new book by Bill Allen contains all the details about the founding of St. Mary's church and the school.

Heading south on the road along the east fence of the cemetery, you will pass through an area of many Chinese and Japanese graves. Both groups have long been in Tulare County. There were

Chinese people listed in the 1860 census, who owned several stores, restaurants and laundries. By 1870 there were three Chinese laundries along the banks of Mill Creek, which was used to wash and rinse clothes and bedding.

The Japanese came here, as many people still do, to work the fields and look for arable land on which to make their own way. There was much anti-Japanese prejudice in the early 1900s. Porterville even had a policy, which it proudly advertised, of "No Japs allowed." However, many settled and farmed, especially in the Dinuba area. Local Japanese families were interned during the Second World War and some were subjected to attacks when they returned after the war. A few families' possessions and land were protected by their neighbors.

East Gate

The east gate ❹ was the original entrance to the five acre cemetery to which 63 more acres have been added over the years. The oldest graves are in this area.

Many early markers were wood. All but a few of these have disappeared over the years. (I could find only one in 1993, illegible and cracked. I could not find this marker in 2010.) Many of them were burned up when the grass was burned off the cemetery, a yearly practice before the advent of mowing. People who could spend more on the funeral had marble markers made. Marble slowly dissolves in water, so many of these very old markers are illegible. I found one from 1855 – one of the graves that was moved in 1860. By 1880 granite replaced marble as the stone

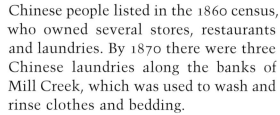

1855 grave

1866 grave

of choice, although there are many other stones used now.

Heading southwest, an amazing natural sight is near Third Street. Locally known as the "Palmolive", this is an olive tree with a California Fan Palm growing right out of the middle of it – they seem to be doing very well together ❺.

Little Lauren

The "Palmolive"

Civil War Memorial

To the north is the Civil War memorial. It was erected in 1916 to honor local people who fought in the Civil War. Visalia, being part of California, was nominally Union, but there were so many Confederate sympathizers here that it was sometimes hard to tell.

At any rate, no official Civil War battles were fought here; the westernmost one was in southern Arizona, where a group of Texan Confederate troops were defeated by Californians at Picacho Peak, fifty miles south of Phoenix.

Children's Graves

Many of the early graves are for children. Typhoid fever, pneumonia, consumption (tuberculosis), malaria, smallpox, the flu, and other diseases took many of them. Often a whole family succumbed to disease in a few weeks.

The markers show that people were not callous about these losses. Each child's death affected them as much as it would us today.

Walk over to the raised brick grave on Second Street ❻. This monument to "Little Lauren" (Holland) who died in 1859 at age four years, seven months, 11 days, says:

A precious one from us has gone,
A voice we loved is stilled
A place is vacant in our home
Which never can be filled.

Before going back to the parking area, head south to the gate. On the way, at 2nd Street, you will pass a large Linden or American Basswood. This species is native to the Northeastern U.S., where it is prized for the shade of its big leaves, its strong but light wood and the honey from its flowers.

Just east of the main entrance is Eagle Niche, a resting place built in 1970 for ashes. Across the street is the Evers Oak ❼, grown from an acorn planted in 1911. It is now about three feet in diameter and more than 60 feet tall.

Room for More

Five hundred forty-five people were buried in the Visalia District Cemetery last year. I asked at the office if they anticipated running out of space, but they said that there is plenty of room now. Some reclaiming has been done – the cemetery taking back unused plots from people who have forgotten about them. This is a difficult and expensive process. Relatives must be searched for; notices published in newspapers country wide; signatures gathered, etc.

A new computer locator program is almost ready to be used by the public. People stopping to visit a relative's grave will be able to type in the name and the computer will identify the location immediately. The written records will still be kept; they are invaluable for their information about dates and places of birth, causes of death, and general demographic statistics.

Stop in and say hello to the nice people who work in the office before you leave.

Dogwood flower

Walk Eight

Highland

This walk is through a magnificent part of old Visalia, with many mature trees and beautiful homes to view. It starts with the new – Highland School, on Stevenson Street between Goshen and Grove ❶, was remodeled in 2008 with a brand new front office and multi-purpose building. This attractive and imposing large building serves as a focal point for the neighborhood now. As you walk north on Stevenson, you will pass one of the original buildings on campus, the small square room that sits at an angle to the street. This was a classroom, built about 1917 when the school was first opened. During its history, Highland has served grades K–8, K–6, K–3, Kindergarten only, and several other configurations.

Map labels: TURNER, JACOB, CONYER, PERSHING, ALLEN, STEVENSON, GROVE, HIGHLAND, WILLIS, WEST, FLORAL, Highland School, Two Oak Park, RACE, GOSHEN, MURRAY, WEST, SCHOOL

Highland School

During the 1980s and 1990s, Highland was the only K–3 school in the Visalia School District. The students transferred to Houston School for grades 4–6, then had to switch again for junior high school. Parents did not like this arrangement, and in 2005 the school district agreed to include grades K–6 again on the Highland campus. The campus is small for this many grades, but local parents are happy to have their children in their neighborhood school for a few more years.

Across from the school is an interesting house with beautiful stained glass and a unique arbor made of grape stakes.

Walk north on Stevenson, then turn left on Grove. The overhanging trees make this area cool, while the vista of the cemetery straight ahead might make one think somber thoughts. Note the nicely kept small homes.

Keep walking past Jacob Street, a wide street with room for bike lanes. A network of bicycle paths and lanes throughout Visalia is encouraged and maintained by the city with the help of interested citizen volunteers who advise the city council. When you get to Turner, along the east edge of the cemetery, turn right for a block to Allen. The large Modesto Ash trees inside the cemetery fence and along the street are full of mistletoe, a parasite that takes advantage of age and weakness in trees. Mistletoe will hurry these trees to their demise.

The east gate of the cemetery ❷ was the original entrance, although I suspect the original east gate was south of here. The oldest graves are to your left as you look in – straight ahead are the Chinese and Japanese sections, and a little to your right is the resting place of George McCann, which is at the edge of "All Hallows," the Catholic section.

819 Pershing Street

Turn right on Allen, then jog north on Conyer Street to Pershing. The small blue house at the corner of Pershing and Stevenson ❸ is dwarfed by the huge Deodar Cedar on the corner. Take a right on Stevenson. The houses are mixed here, mostly early California bungalows with some Queen Anne style. Attractive fences abound, all different. A left on Grove takes you down another beautiful street.

On the NW corner of Grove and Highland is an old home with a clinker brick chimney (left). In the summer of 2008 the owner noticed a buzzing sound in the wall around this chimney.

807 N. Highland Street

Watching, he noticed some bees busily entering and exiting through small cracks in the siding. A beekeeper came and removed the hive, but there may still be some honey inside the walls. Across Highland is a Spanish style house with a round, columned porch – quite an eclectic mix of styles (below).

722 Willis Street

810 Highland Street

Keep heading east on Grove to Willis ❹. Note the beautiful homes, some in need of restoration, along here. The mature plantings add to their grandeur. Look down Willis Street, or if you have time, turn and stroll to the right (south) down this beautiful avenue of stately homes. 500 W. Grove, on the corner, is a Craftsman bungalow built about 1915 with a pop-up second story and decorated with clinker brick.

714 Willis Street

Keep going to Floral Street and turn right. 733 Floral is a Craftsman style home with a great porch that shows the Prairie style influences, built about 1910 ❺.

733 Floral Street

500 W. Grove Avenue

It's fun to think about how people lived here 100 years ago. The new technologies were the first motorized vehicles and the telegraph was the main means of long distance communication. News of the Wright brothers' flight reached Visalia soon after it happened, and by 1910 cars were becoming common. The telephone had just arrived and was used for local calls. In agriculture, portable water pumps made irrigation more efficient. The first tractors were doing the work of oxen and horses. George Washington Carver and other scientists were learning about what makes plants grow. The benefit of nitrogen to the soil was discovered in the mid 1800s, and fertilizers were starting to be manufactured and transported. Crops were irrigated using dams and canals. Doctors and veterinarians could cure many diseases and were starting to understand how germs spread. The first antibiotic was developed in 1909 and was widely distributed quickly. Dairies and farms were becoming more efficient for all of these reasons.

Cross Race Avenue and continue to Goshen Avenue. The house across from the florist, 601 W. Goshen, is the Murray house ❻. A. H. Murray and his family settled in Tulare County in the mid 1800s. This is one of the earliest homes in Visalia, but this is not its original location – it was moved from the namesake Murray Avenue in 1979.

Zig-zag back to the northwest. Going north on Willis toward Race, you pass under two large avocado trees. In late summer through the autumn, you can often find these delicious fruits on the ground unless neighborhood kids have already picked them up.

The Labyrinth

These avocados are in the yard of the house that was known until recently as the "House of Chan" ❼. Gay Chan moved to Visalia in 1929 and started a grocery store on Locust Street just north of Main, which was in business until he retired in 1970. He and his wife lived in this house in retirement. Gay Chan's daughter, Lori Luna, and her husband now live here and have recently taken out the lawn to put in drought tolerant plants and a labyrinth for a meditative space. Note the Wisteria that have been trained to climb the fence. On the east side of the front of this beautiful home

Murray House

House of Chan

are a huge Pomelo tree and an enormous ginkgo. The house was built about 1916 for Carrie Elliott, daughter of the Thomas family who owned much of the land around here.

Across Race Avenue is the first apartment house in Visalia, 700 N. Willis Street, with 6 units built about 1925.

A Coast Redwood and a California Fan Palm flank the front walk, reminding us of our state's natural diversity.

Head west on Race one block to Highland. The home on the bend in the road here has a new boxwood hedge. Boxwood grows slowly but thickly. Its many small leaves define shapes well. It

Apartment House at 700 N. Willis Street

Trained Wisteria

is the plant of choice for English garden hedges and is used often for topiaries. It will take a few years for this hedge to fill in, but when it does the owner will have a beautiful border around his home.

Two Oak Park

Look north on Highland to Two Oak Park ❽, one of the smaller city parks. In 1910 this 30 feet wide by 70 feet long park was proposed by the surveyor of the area to protect the two large Valley Oaks it contains. Its official name is Highland Park. See if you can find the concrete marker, placed in 1914 on the site. Terry Ommen's book, *Visalia Then and Now*, contains a picture of this park soon after

it was established. There are now four Valley Oaks on this little island, but the two large ones stand out. The growths on the trunks, seen on many oaks, are burls, areas of convoluted grain caused usually by some injury to the trunk. Burls of some trees are prized for their grain by wood workers, but Valley Oak is so hard to work with that even the burls are not much used.

One more block brings you back to Highland School. For more information about the beautiful homes in this part of Visalia, get a copy of *Visalia's Heritage: Buildings, People, History*, available from the Tulare County Historical Society and in the library.

Highland, or "Two Oak" Park

Walk Nine

Beverly Glen

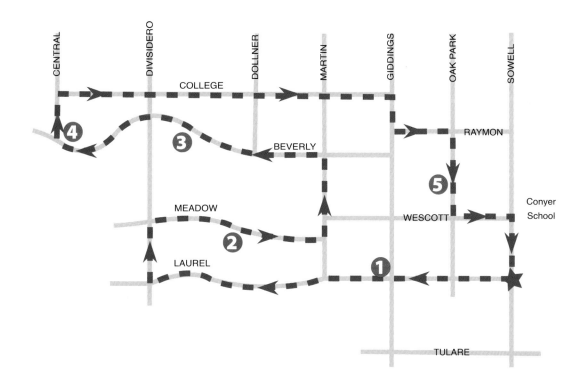

This walk goes through a neighborhood of winding streets and expensive, well-kept homes. Beverly Glen was developed in the early 1960s, when it was on the outskirts of Visalia. The College of the Sequoias had been established in 1956 out in the country on Mooney Boulevard, and this development filled in some of the gap between the city and the college. We start on Sowell Street, just north of Tulare, heading west on Laurel. These houses were built in the 1940s and 50s, before Beverly Glen, which really starts at Giddings Street.

Notice the mature plantings all along this walk. The large trees, especially the oaks, add a lot to the atmosphere of this neighborhood. Visalia's status as a tree city and the Oak Tree Protection Ordinance here really make neighborhoods desirable. At the corner of Laurel and Sowell are a large Weeping Willow and two Coast Redwoods. Farther along are two large magnolias on the south side of the street and a birch tree on the north. This street marks the start of the nice, large, independently-designed houses that give the Beverly Glen area its character. Note that many of the shake roofs are in poor shape. They will be replaced with another type of roof soon as wood shake roofs are no longer allowed because of the fire danger.

Laurelwood

As you enter Beverly Glen you will see "Laurelwood," the imposing brick house on the corner ❶. The beautiful huge oak trees in the yard, the ornamentation on the house, the widow's walk and the dormer window in front with a railing above it, all combine to make this the perfect place for weddings and similar parties. In fact, the house was purchased in 2006 with that in mind. But the new owners had not checked with the city or with the neighbors, who protested effectively about the potential parking and congestion problems. Now Laurelwood is for sale again, but only as a small but stately residence. Behind the house on the west you can see a pointed pole sticking up from a sort of gazebo-like structure. This is the belfry which was

removed from Jefferson School when it was torn down in 1954 (See Walk #1).

Just west of Laurelwood, hidden behind large Coast Redwoods, is a home that is the essence of the 1960s with redwood siding, large plate glass windows, and a near A-frame shape. The owners actually wanted to build an A-frame but the city would not let them, so the architect designed it as close to that shape as he could. Inside is a soaring beamed ceiling over a two-story living room. A spiral staircase leads to a loft above the kitchen. The east wall is all glass, which lightens the natural redwood paneling throughout. This house was inserted between its neighbors on a small lot, and was finished in 1969.

Across the street and a little farther west, 1407 W. Laurel is an attractive home with simple lines. The large Silver Maple is a beautiful tree, with its low hanging branches. Note the duck topiary in the bush by the driveway. The owner of the house must be a duck hunter or perhaps a birdwatcher.

1515 W. Meadow

The plantings all along this street are superb, but the next house stands out. No grassy areas; instead the front is planted with ground covers and shrubs, beautiful in winter and blossoming all spring and summer.

Head to Divisadero Street and turn north. As you walk down busy streets you will quickly become aware of the lack of sidewalks. Visalia now has an ordinance which requires developers to install sidewalks, but in the 1950s and 1960s they did not. Visalia's growth has allowed it to become a more planned city in some ways; there is now an official city council sponsored volunteer committee that recommends improvements to sidewalks and bicycle trails.

At the Corner of Divisadero and Meadow is a Colorado Blue Spruce. This, the state tree of Colorado, grows high in the Rocky Mountains, and survives in this desert reluctantly. Turn east here on Meadow.

Wright-like House

1515 W. Meadow ❷ is a striking home that was designed by a student of Frank Lloyd Wright, Robert Campbell, who lived and worked in Three Rivers in the 1950s. He built this home with its low metal roof and front circular window in 1955. The owner has kept the house visible by not planting trees in front, emphasizing the simple straight lines of the design. Across the street, Siberian Elms shade a more typical Visalia home.

In the next block is a miniature orange grove. Both Navels and Valencias grow well here in Visalia, and if you plant one of each you will have plenty of fresh orange juice almost year-round. Keep walking to Martin Street, where you will notice on the north side a large home on a huge lot – the front yard is much larger than others in the area, as is the back yard. The original owner may have purchased two lots and combined them, or there may have been an existing house here situated so that this lot could not easily be divided.

Across Martin is a beautifully landscaped home with a garage behind it. This garage has been rebuilt recently because a few years ago a two foot diameter branch fell from the oak tree next to it, crushing the roof and one side of the building. The owners are very careful to keep their oak trees pruned after that surprise.

Straight Streets

We are zigzagging through the neighborhood – go north on Martin one block to Beverly, then west again. Enjoy the unique houses. The roof of the house on the corner of Beverly and Martin is truly amazing, with its high peaks and many angles. The large Valley Oaks around some houses give a stately feel as well as much shade. A large Loquat juts out over the sidewalk, but is trimmed so you can walk under it.

Interesting plantings around here: A huge Valley Oak in the yard of the hacienda style house at 1409 Beverly. Three large sycamores are across the street at the corner of Beverly and Dollner. To the west a yard full of roses with a big Coast Redwood and another large oak. Also some more interesting architecture: a Spanish style home with a turret over the entryway is across from a two-story Tudor style home ❸. Each house is unique in this neighborhood.

Cross Divisadero heading west and find a beautiful Spanish style home ❹.

1520 Beverly Ave.

The yard is planted in drought-tolerant plants, with a fig tree in the corner of the yard to add color and sweetness. Figs do not use much water once established, and the fruit attracts birds as well as humans. Turn north on Central.

From College Street north the streets are straight. When my children were little, they told the difference in neighborhoods by this one symptom. They often asked me why we couldn't live in a neighborhood with crooked streets. But the houses on College, Myrtle, and Kaweah are still grand and interesting.

1520 College St.

1520 College is a false timbered Tudor style with fun windows that have curved dormer roofs over them. Also note the large Century Plant (a kind of agave) on the south side of the street. This plant will grow until it flowers – which can be 20 years or more, but probably not a full century. After flowering it dies, but many small plants spring up from its base to begin the cycle again. There are hundreds of varieties of agave. Some kinds were an important source of food and water for stranded desert travelers, and several kinds are farmed in Mexico

Spanish style home at the corner of
Myrtle and Martin Streets

the trees meeting over the middle. Turn south, then east again on Raymon. Note the smaller homes, even a duplex or two. These houses also have smaller lots and are more standard-issue, with less custom design. Turn south on Oak Park.

There are a few interesting design features apparent here. Check out the undulating block wall in front of 915 S. Oak Park ❺. This wall was built as insurance against a flood. The square openings can be easily and quickly filled with sand bags if needed. Someone went

for the sweet pulp that is fermented into tequila and mescal.

As you head east, see how friendly Divisadero Street feels with the trees in the middle. Sometime in the 1990s some of these trees died as a result of a gas pipe leaking under them. After the gas company repaired the leak, the city replaced the Valley Oaks, which have grown well but are smaller than the rest of this urban forest.

Keep going east on College Avenue to Giddings, another friendly street, with

to a lot of extra work to make this wall serpentine, though. Always keep your eyes open for surprises – I see new things every time I walk around these neighborhoods.

Turn left on Wescott and head back to your car. Conyer School, just to the north on Sowell, was originally built on the other side of the playground, facing Conyer Street, in 1922. It was a K–3 school for years but is now, like all Visalia Unified elementary schools, kindergarten through grade six. In 1947 the present main building was constructed and the old school torn down. The commemorative wall that stands outside the main entrance is made from bricks from the original school.

You have just walked about two miles through a beautiful neighborhood.

Under the street

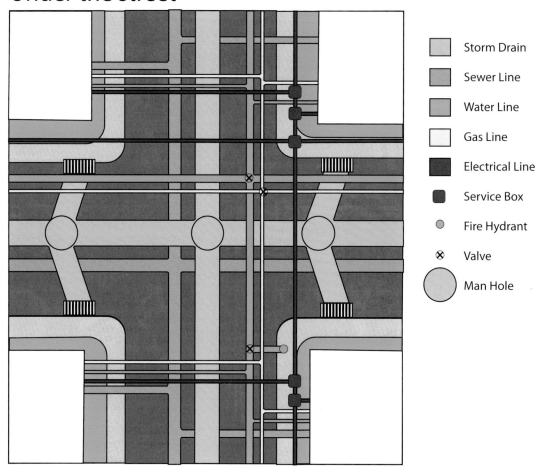

▢	Storm Drain
▢	Sewer Line
▢	Water Line
▢	Gas Line
▢	Electrical Line
▪	Service Box
●	Fire Hydrant
⊗	Valve
◯	Man Hole

Profile

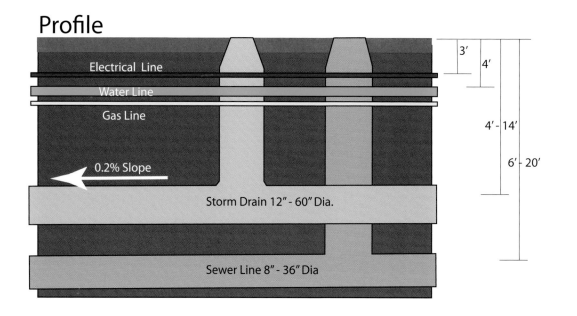

Electrical Line

Water Line

Gas Line

0.2% Slope

Storm Drain 12" - 60" Dia.

Sewer Line 8" - 36" Dia

3'

4'

4' - 14'

6' - 20'

Looking Down

Pavement and What's Underneath

Like all cities, Visalia has grown in spurts and under different political climates. Regulations have played a large part in how the city has grown, as has advancement in technology and building techniques. Various city ordinances, state laws, and simple agreements with developers have played a role in the manner in which the city's services have been supplied.

Sidewalks

Sidewalks are one example. Sidewalks were expected along all streets until after World War II, when rapid growth and the fact that nearly everyone had a car made them seem superfluous. Now, as we strive to make it possible to use cars less, we have again required sidewalks in new developments.

In the 1800s, Visalia was dusty, dirty, and often muddy. Mill Creek and the other distributaries of the Kaweah ran almost year-round and overflowed the banks regularly. Pedestrians shared the streets with horses and carriages pulled by horses, mules, and oxen. The first wooden sidewalks were installed by store owners in the 1850s. The first bridge crossed Mill Creek in 1865, creating what is still called Bridge Street. Some Visalia streets were paved in the late 1860s with gravel hand-mined from the river beds and with a material they found in the foothills that is still used today – decomposed granite. When wetted down

and compacted, decomposed granite, or D.G. as it is called, becomes relatively hard and dust free. Later, concrete and asphalt were used as they are today.

There are still many sidewalks from the 1910s and 1920s around town. Although concrete generally gets tougher as it ages, many older sidewalks were poorly constructed and they are crumbling. The underlayment is cheap concrete, made with less cement than is needed. It's less than two inches thick. On top is one half inch or less of smooth slurry (cement-sand mixture.) The foundation crumbles and the top flakes off. You can find these sidewalks wherever there are older homes.

With sidewalks and paved streets, curbs were needed to separate the two. The first curbs were made of hard granite

Granite Curb with original horse ring in downtown Visalia

mined in the mountains and brought here. Some of these are still lining Main, Locust, Church, and Court Streets in the downtown area. There are a few horse rings still installed in these granite curbs – keep a sharp eye out for them as you go on downtown walks.

Poured concrete curbs were the standard from the early 1900s until the 1950s, when rolled curbs came into vogue. Rolled curbs allowed builders to use the same curb configuration all the way across a property and not have to change to a driveway cut. However, they do not define driveways well and modern cars with low clearance bottom out on them. Curbs of today are more like the original granite curbs, but they are angled away from the street and are constructed low enough for a pickup to drive over when needed. Driveways are well defined by ramped cuts.

Bicycles are an important form of transportation. When Acequia Avenue was changed from one-way to two-way in 2009, a controversy arose over putting

bike lanes on Acequia. Some businesses were sure that street parking was needed, while bicycle commuters held that there were no safe bike paths through the downtown area. The new parking garages were built to help relieve street parking issues, and Acequia got bike lanes. The City of Visalia Waterways and Trails committee is a volunteer group that is

commissioned to help make these decisions. This group also places the new bike racks around town like the ones by the Fox Theatre and Bank of America. The purpose is to encourage alternatives to cars and to make Visalia accessible for bicyclists and pedestrians.

Street Striping

The stripes on the streets are sprayed on as needed for traffic separation and safety. Most smaller residential streets have no stripes, but larger streets have lane separation lines and crosswalk stripes. The paint is either a thick latex paint, specially designed for durability and fast drying, or sometimes a thermoplastic that is heated like nacho cheese as it is applied. Both paints are infused with small glass beads that increase the reflective qualities of the paint. Many stripes are enhanced by epoxied-on reflectors that reflect oncoming light. These reflectors stick up about one-half inch, just enough to appear above a light-reflecting puddle after a rain storm and to provide a warning bump to cars that cross the line. The city hires striping companies to put paint on streets. These crews usually work late at night or very early in the morning so the paint can dry before heavy traffic. A truck follows the paint truck, just far enough behind to let the paint dry and keep any traffic off it for ten minutes or so.

Eric Bons, city traffic engineer, recalled a phone call he received one day. A young man said there was paint all over his truck from some fresh street painting. Luckily, the striping company had called earlier and told him about a truck that had been swerving between the paint truck and the follower truck, running over the fresh paint again and again at 2:00 AM. Eric asked if the truck was a silver Ford 4×4. The man said it was, and Eric referred him to the striping company, saying that they were responsible for damage.

When the driver called the striping company, they told him to come down and make a statement, "and the police will be here to hear what you have to say." That ended the matter.

Fire Hydrants

Fire hydrants are connected to water mains by 6 inch diameter pipes. They are designed so that a full stream of water at pressure is available with a quick turn of the valve. Since fire hoses carried by city trucks are 150 feet long, hydrants are no more than 300 feet apart. The hydrant is connected to the pipe with shear bolts – these are made to break off if the hydrant is hit, so as to minimize damage to the plumbing in the ground. There is no check valve, though, so a sheared hydrant results in quite a fountain until someone can come and shut the valve, which is usually under a small cover in the street where the hydrant connects to the main.

Hydrants are owned by California Water Service, the company that supplies our water here in Visalia. New hydrants cost about $1,000 and installation costs add another $2,000–5,000 to that. Although they do not charge for the water used on a fire, they may charge you for the water spilled if you knock a hydrant off its base, plus $400 or so to re-install, and the cost of replacement if needed. Sometimes hydrants survive getting hit by a car, but usually they are damaged beyond repair. (Thanks to Mike Makarian for the information about water service and fire hydrants.)

Manhole Covers

The round covers we see on many streets are properly called sewer grates, although "manhole cover" is universally used. Sewer grates have been in use since sewers were invented – stone grates can be found on aqueducts from Roman times. Their purpose is to provide ventilation, especially air to replace the air displaced by moving sewer water, and to give access to the pipes for inspection and repair.

Manhole covers need to be heavy, so they are made of cast iron and weigh about 100 pounds. Most are 25½″ in diameter and cover a 24″ shaft. They have a texture so they are not too slippery when wet. They are best when round because they cannot fall in the hole – a rectangular one could fall through on the diagonal. They are also round because the shafts they cover are usually round; a round shape is best for resisting crushing forces from all sides. They are heavy to prevent people from picking them up, although low slung race cars traveling very fast can loosen them – in France they weld down the covers before the Lemans road race. The small holes in the covers are for venting and also to insert a pick with which a worker can move the cover out of the way when service is required.

Star-studded covers are common in older parts of Visalia

Covers provide access to the four chief pipes running under city streets. The largest pipes are storm drains, 12″ to 60″ diameter, which gather water from gutters and dump it in settling basins and waterways throughout the city. Drains must be sized so that they are never more than half full. If too full, they could vacuum lock and stop the water from moving, like a straw with your finger over the end. On the corner of two large streets you will often see two covers over the trunk line where the street drains on each corner empty into it. There is an access point with a manhole cover over it at every junction of two storm drain pipes. Trunk lines are at least six feet deep throughout the city.

The next smaller pipes are sanitary sewers, which drain house waste including toilets and water borne waste from industrial plants. The manhole covers are still 25½ inches in diameter, of course, because they must be large enough for a person to enter. The sanitary sewer pipes that run throughout the city are 8″ to 36″ in diameter, and again must be sized so that they are never more than half full.

The third covers in the streets are usually small – 12″ in diameter. These are over junctions in water mains (sometimes

1½ inch gas pipe with valves in front of a 3 inch water check valve that serve large buildings

gas pipes, too), and 4 feet or more under each cover is one or more valves that can be turned to control flow throughout the city. California Water company workers use a special wrench with an eight foot handle to reach the valves through the holes under the small covers.

At the top of the opening under every manhole cover is a grade ring, which is lined up with the pavement and holds the cover. When a street is repaved, a second grade ring may have to be added to keep the cover at street level.

Water mains are 8–12 inches in diameter throughout the city. Many different materials have been used over the years for water mains, from cast iron to cement lined with fiber. Now most mains are ductile steel or PVC plastic pipes. Steel pipes supply house water from the mains. House water is pressurized at 40–60 psi, so slope is not a concern. The pressure is supplied by pumps which are on the wells throughout the system and are programmed to deliver constant pressure. When demand is very high, such as at 5–6 AM on a typical weekday when everyone in Visalia is taking a shower, the storage tanks at Redwood High and other places are called on to supplement the water supplied by wells.

When you see pipes with valves above ground they are usually backflow prevention valves for a fire suppression system in a commercial building. Gas valves may also have a check valve feature on commercial buildings.

Various other covers are used for access to electrical and communications cables. These are usually in the sidewalks. Larger covers may lead to underground vaults – such as the ones that house the controls for the lights at major intersections – or to a splice in the cables that may need repair at some point. These underground vaults must also be vented to prevent the buildup of toxic gases, heat, and condensation. The vents are perforated pipes that stick up three feet through sidewalks.

Vents in sidewalk for an Edison vault. Entrance to the vault is through the manhole cover behind them.

Communications boxes (telephone and cable) are usually above ground and behind the sidewalks in out-of-the-way corners of yards. Some large boxes extend several feet underground and have fans running all the time to keep the equipment inside cool.

Slope

All drains must slope downhill, and Visalia is on a very gradual (0.2%) slope downhill to the west, toward the sewage treatment plant just southwest of the junction of 198 and 99. The gradual slope is important. If the slope ever gets steeper than 3% or so, the water leaves the solids behind in the pipe and that can cause blockage. In cities on hills, pipes are set to be either close to level or very steep, never just gradual at 3–30% slope – that would cause blockage.

Waste sewer trunk lines are up to 18 feet deep to preserve the low slope. The deepest lines in the city are in the area of the new sports park on Highway 63. If they were not deep on the northeast edge of the city, the slope would be too great. From there the waste drains slope gradually to the pumping station near the airport, where all of Visalia's sewage is gathered together into two 48" diameter pipes that are pressurized to push the waste under Highway 99 and on to the treatment plant.

The storm sewers do not drain to the treatment plant. Instead the water collected is put into the various streams and ditches that run throughout Visalia, and from there filter through sand and earth to groundwater. In some places there are pumps that push storm water into the ground for recharge of groundwater supplies. This is one reason it is very important not to put used motor oil

Large wires carry high voltage to the transformer on the left side. The right side wires distribute low voltage current to users.

Electric transformers are often above ground, too. Southern California Edison places these boxes in out of the way places, painted olive green. Inside are the high voltage wires on one side and the low voltage (household current) on the other. Electricity moves through wires more efficiently at high voltage. The transformer changes the incoming voltage to 220 and 120 volt that is needed for home and most business use.

A telephone system distribution box.

or left over insecticides into the storm system. They are also poor choices to pour down the drain into the sanitary sewer – take them to the hazardous waste drop off.

Curb Sewers

Storm sewers are only under major streets. Other streets use the curbs to gather storm water and direct it to the sewer system. When a curb drain crosses a street, there are two choices. One is to create a dip for the water to run through and cars to go over. This is not very popular with drivers, and there are only a few of these in Visalia. (The dip on Terrace Street just south of Walnut catches me every time!) The other is to build a cross drain. This is a pipe that goes from the high side of a cross street to the lower side. An entrance grate on the high side and an exit grate on the lower side allow water to cross under the street and appear again in the gutter on the other side.

These cross drains have a few problems. First, they only hide the water that is flowing under the street; they do not

Cross drain exit grating

get rid of it. It builds up on its slow trip downhill until it reaches an impasse – a clogged drain or a low spot – and there it can puddle. Also, people do not realize that the cross drains do not connect to the sewer. They call the street department after each heavy rain to complain about the water coming out of the grate on the downhill side. There is a more important problem, though, and that is that every one of these cross drains contains standing water, and standing water is where mosquitoes breed in warm weather. In addition to the nuisance, mosquitoes spread disease. Until the early 1900s malaria was prevalent in Visalia. The mosquito that carries the malaria parasite has been eradicated here, but there are other problem mosquitoes here. Two of the most common species here are *Culex quinquefasciatus*, the Southern House Mosquito, which carries West Nile virus and *Culex tarsalis*, which carries West Nile and encephalitis.

Since 1922 part of our property taxes in Visalia has supported Delta Vector Control. From May through October, trucks go around the city looking for places mosquitoes might breed. Workers toss pellets of methoprene into the cross drains. This chemical confuses second and third larval stage mosquitoes and causes them to stop their development. Methoprene is non-toxic to mammals and birds.

As you walk around Visalia, look down. There may be an important pipe several feet below you.

By California standards traffic is light in Visalia. The intersection of Demaree and Walnut (pictured here) was the busiest in town 20 years ago

Traffic

Controlling Drivers

The first automobile that arrived in Visalia was most likely a steam Locomobile, driven here along the wagon trails in 1898. Harry Brown, the owner of the car, was driving it around the state looking for investors. By about 1902 there were several steam and one-cylinder gas cars in town.

Visalia even had an automobile factory briefly. Brother mechanics Morton and Billy Thompson, who worked for the Dudley's carriage and harness shop, created three automobiles before the growing factories in Detroit took all the business. The Cadillac agency sold its first car to the lumberman William R. Spalding in 1907. The Spaldings renovated their carriage house to accommodate this car and Mrs. Spalding's Baker electric car.

It's amazing to think that people had cars here in those days. The roads were terrible. In the 1910s the intersection of State Highway 198 and 99 was two dirt roads crossing. Horse drawn carts had trouble when it rained. Early automobiles, with thin tires and little power, had to be pulled out with teams of horses or oxen, the farmers laughing at the rich folks' folly all the while.

However, there was great excitement about cars in the early days. As early as 1912 Visalia was a center for automobile racing. That summer, over 50,000 people showed up to watch a race through downtown Visalia. The winning car of

A brand new Cleveland Automobile is stuck along Highway 99 in 1907. Photo from the *Visalia Times-Delta* February 1, 1954.

the 16 that signed up for the race was a National, averaging 48 miles per hour for the 150 mile, 48 lap race. The course was Main Street to Giddings, south to Tulare, then east to Garden to return to Main Street.

Traffic Lights

The first traffic lights in the world were put into use in the mid 1800s in London, where a gas light, red on one side and green the other, helped control buggies and horses on the busy streets. It was turned by a man who held it in the middle of the street. One exploded in 1869, injuring the operator.

It was in the U.S. that the electric traffic light got its start in 1920. William Potts of Detroit, Michigan is credited with inventing the three-color, four directional signal we use today. Potts was a police officer who probably thought of it while he was standing in the middle of an intersection all day. In 1923 Garrett Morgan of Cleveland, Ohio patented a traffic signal that was an extension of and an improvement on Potts's ideas. Morgan was the first African-American to own an automobile in Cleveland and the inventor of many useful things, such as the gas mask. By the end of the 1920s, traffic signals were used everywhere.

We haven't yet found out when the first traffic lights were installed along Main Street. Pictures from the 1930s show them while some earlier pictures do not, so it was sometime in the late 1920s to early 1930s. There is plenty of research that is needed to be done in old *Times-Delta* newspapers for this kind of arcane fact.

In 2009 it cost at least $250,000 to install lights at an existing intersection where two four-lane streets meet, more if left- or right-hand turn lanes and lights are added. Each intersection requires at least 8 poles, 4 or more of them with arms that hang over the street – these cost $25,000 to $40,000 each, installed. Add to that all the hardware and wiring. Traffic light intersections also have pedestrian lights and the controls that go with them. New installations must include a 4–6 hour battery powered backup. Lights require electrical conduit to be placed under the roadways in all directions. The digital controls are housed in a large steel box mounted on the sidewalk on one corner. Each intersection is individually designed by an engineer in Visalia's Traffic Safety Division.

The widening of Mooney Boulevard from 2 lanes to 3 in 2009–2010 required CalTrans to install new traffic signals at

New lights being installed next to the old during Mooney Blvd. widening

all the intersections. These new poles have 65 ft. long arms, to reach from the far side of the sidewalk all the way to the left turn lane, holding the bottom of the lights at the required height of 17 feet above the roadway. As construction proceeds, new control boxes are built and conduit is extended under the pavement.

In Visalia the Traffic Safety Division keeps a prioritized list of intersections that may need traffic lights. The engineers there monitor these intersections and dole out their limited funds as they can to upgrade. At this writing (2009), Visalia has about 140 intersections controlled by traffic lights. About 35 of these are owned by the state – on Mooney, Court and Locust, Dinuba Boulevard., Mineral King, and Noble. 105 are owned by the city.

Until the mid 1980s, eight inch diameter incandescent fixtures were the norm. Some ten inch fixtures were used on larger streets. Some eight inch fixtures still are in use in Visalia, but you should hurry to see them because replacement is planned. At the corner of Mineral King and Giddings, the sidewalk poles have eight inch lights while the ones hanging over the middle of the intersection on arms have a twelve inch red light over the two eight inch yellow and green.

Eight-inch diameter lights
on Mineral King at Giddings

Twelve-inch diameter red light
over two eights

Each of the bulbs in a new light fixture is 12 inches in diameter and uses LED technology, 90% to 95% more energy efficient than the equivalent brightness incandescent bulb.

100–160 watt incandescent bulbs (left)
have been replaced almost everywhere
by 8–12 watt LED arrays (right)

Red was the first color to be available in LED arrays, starting in the early 1990s. Since red lights are on more than all others, changing them would save the most electricity. The price was prohibitively high at first, but has been going down since they were invented. Visalia began installing red LED bulbs in about 1995, and followed with green as the price came down. Many yellows are still incandescent as of this writing, but they will be changed out over the next few years through a program sponsored by Southern California Edison. Each LED bulb costs about $50.00 now (2009). They draw 8–10 watts instead of the 100–160 watt incandescent lights that were used before. Still, with at least twelve bulbs on at all times, an average intersection uses several hundred dollars a year in electricity.

LED bulbs have changed over the years they have been available. The first generation bulbs were arrays of small LED bulbs that each emitted the color of light needed. New ones have 1 or 2 larger LED emitters and draw only about 8 watts. The lens is either colored or clear, depending on the preference of the buyer. Lenses are made of high impact,

First generation LED traffic light

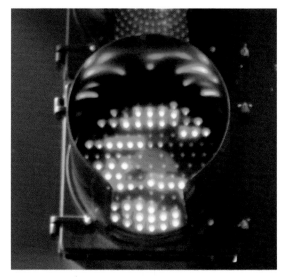

A CalTrans light shows "lights out" patterns.

UV stabilized polycarbonate which is tested to withstand 60 months facing south in direct Arizona sunlight without yellowing. The lenses are designed to emit light directionally, so only approaching drivers can see it. You can see both clear and colored lenses in Visalia. Clear lenses do not show the color of the light when it is off.

Besides being cheaper to operate, LED bulbs are bright for 5–10 years instead of the 1–2 years that the specially made incandescent bulbs last. This saves lots of money, not only in electricity charges, but also in the cost of the equipment and person hours to put new ones in. LEDs are safer because they dim gradually rather than just go out, giving warning and time to replace them, and they are brighter, especially in bright sunlight. Old style LED bulbs fail in patterns, and are supposed to be replaced when 25% of the individual bulbs are out. Red bulbs are replaced before that for safety reasons, but green is often left longer. New style LED bulbs fade gradually, and are recommended to be replaced after 5 years.

Almost all lights have a visor that shades the bulb so it is more visible in

sunlight. New visors do not have bottoms so that birds cannot build nests inside them and block the light. I guess it took a smart engineer to think of that because older lights had this problem sometimes. Some lights are very directional and cannot be seen except in the lane they control. This is done either by baffles inside the visors or by special directional lenses.

Timing the Lights

Until the 1980s, intersections were controlled by mechanical timers something like old-fashioned sprinkler controls. They were full of gears, cams, bearings, wires, etc. They were remarkably reliable, but required experts to repair them when they did break. Digital timers are

A traffic light control box with battery backup

used now. Timers are a plug-in module and are replaced if they malfunction (which happens rarely). Maintenance people program the timers by plugging in to them as needed. Some can be programmed remotely.

Both sides of the control box can open, revealing the modules that can be replaced (left) and the wires that connect them (right)

The length of time each color is on depends on the legal speed of the traffic on the streets meeting at the intersection. Green and red vary from 15–40 seconds, while the yellow is on for 3–8 seconds. After the yellow there is a 1 second delay when all sides are red – this is a safety measure against both yellow light runners and eager green jumpers. A circuit called a conflict monitor provides an electrical barrier that prevents green lights appearing in both directions. If a problem occurs, such as might happen if a pole is knocked over or as a result of an electrical outage, all lights default to flashing red until someone resets the intersection. In most cases when the power goes off, the battery back-up system takes control of the lights so quickly that no interruption is perceived by drivers or even by the digital controller. When power is restored, there is again no glitch in service.

Most of Visalia's traffic signal intersections are linked in networks that cover areas of the city. About a third of the lights are controlled by a central computer that times the lights to accommodate the traffic and keep it moving. To set up a timing schedule, traffic through intersections is analyzed and timed and a theory is formulated by city engineers. Then they try it out and see what happens, adjusting the timing as needed until they have the most traffic continuously moving.

Although it seems that it would make sense to time all the lights on one street together, this can't be done practically. There are so many intersections that a traveler on any of the north-south streets would be stopped by nearly every crossing if everything was timed for east-west travel. Therefore, sets of lights are timed together to keep traffic moving in the direction most people go, but you can always count on having to stop somewhere. The exceptions are the CalTrans streets. CalTrans controls the lights on their streets, such as Mooney Boulevard, and their system is not completely compatible with Visalia's. Their streets are the biggest and most important, so the timing of the lights on Mooney, Court, Locust, Noble, and Mineral King has priority over the smaller streets controlled by the city.

When traffic is light, intersections are controlled mostly by approaching traffic. A wire placed an inch or so under the pavement creates an inductive loop. When a vehicle, from a bicycle to a bulldozer, passes over the loop, the magnetic field is interrupted. This difference in the field is translated electronically into the turning of a switch to change the light. The sensitivity of the loop can be adjusted so that a crow will not trip it, but a child on a bike will. There are times in the cycle and times of the day when this on demand feature is turned off.

Two other things control traffic lights. One is pedestrians, who can push a button and cause the traffic to stop. If it seems that the buttons do not work, that is usually because the light is at a time in its cycle when it cannot be interrupted. The other controllers of signals are emergency vehicles. Police cars, fire trucks, and ambulances are equipped with invisible strobe lights that preempt the control of lights. So far about half of the lights in Visalia are equipped with the receiving device.

Even though there seem to be thousands of drivers here who think yellow means go, Visalia has no red light cameras. There is much controversy about the use of them in this country, the main problem being that charges are against the driver, not the vehicle, and it is hard for a camera to see inside the vehicle well enough to identify who is at the wheel. Other countries just send the ticket to the vehicle's owner and let them sort it out.

Stop Signs

Stop signs are the option for streets with less traffic. They cost about $50 per sign and the city orders them in lots of 100–200 signs. They wear out, and the ones that face south fade the fastest, needing to be replaced every four or five years. Some are graffitied; some are bent by motorists.

Stop signs can be refurbished once or twice before the aluminum is too thin and must be recycled. Visalia's signs are sent to a business that grinds off the surface and replaces the laminated reflective red and white "stop." Then an anti-graffiti coating is applied and the sign is as good as new.

A four-way stop is often safer than an intersection with a light because both directions are asked to stop, so if one driver forgets, the other will probably compensate. A safety comparison is difficult, though, because of relative traffic volume. Cities cannot afford to stop traffic in both directions at every intersection – it slows traffic too much, as you can see if you have ever been at a blinking red intersection at a busy time of day.

Thanks for the information about Visalia's traffic lights goes to Eric Bons, Senior Civil Engineer of the City of Visalia Traffic Safety Division, and Brian Motl, Senior Traffic Signal Technician.

Looking Up

Trees, Birds, Mountains

> *. . . there is a harmony*
> *In Autumn, and a lustre in its sky*
> *Which through the summer is not heard or seen.*
>
> – Percy Bysshe Shelley

Autumn Color

Autumn comes late to Visalia, but when the cold weather finally arrives, the colors of the hundreds of species of trees here rival anything New England has to offer. Couple that with clear weather that allows the mountains to reveal themselves, and you might think that Shelley visited Visalia before he wrote the lines above. Stroll down any street in town and look around. The trees may not be as densely massed together as they are in Eastern forests, but nowhere can match our variety.

Many of the trees that grow here are evergreen. The shapely Camphor trees hang on to their dark green leaves all winter along with the dark berries that feed migrating birds. Evergreen magnolias are less dense, but still glossy and bright. Eucalyptus keep their distinctive gray-green leaves. The dark green of the citrus, hanging now with colorful fruit, complements the bright colors of neighboring deciduous trees.

The showiest of the deciduous trees is the Liquidambar, or Sweetgum tree. I have had little good to say about this tree in previous chapters, but at this time of the year the Liquidambar's sins

Liquidambar tree in Visalia yard

are almost forgiven. The dense leaves turn from medium green to burgundy, with golden highlights, and stay on the tree for several weeks before falling off a dull brown. The trees vary individually; it is best to pick one at the nursery in the fall so you know what colors it will turn. However, individual trees vary from year to year, and even from branch to branch. The south side seems to color up the best, but that also depends on location, neighboring trees, and many other factors.

Also dark red are some of the flowering pears, which seem to retain much green for contrast. Each leaf changes in circular stripes from green to red. Look for stray white blossoms this time of year; sometimes the variable autumn weather triggers flowering in many fruits.

Bright foliage can be found on Chinese Pistache trees, like the ones outside the library. Some of these trees turn nearly pink, others dark purple.

Ginkgo

Pistache Tree

Yellow is the most common color family, with shades varying from orange to chartreuse. Ginkgoes and Tulip Poplar trees both become bright yellow, as do the trees in the poplar family like the Fremont Cottonwoods along Mill Creek. This makes the clumps of green mistletoe stand out in contrast just in time for Christmas. Try not to get your feet too wet while standing under it.

Tulip Tree or Tulip Poplar

ashes are small now; by spring they will be ready to fly.

Valley Oaks just turn from their dusty green to a dusty brown, but the leaves fall and leave behind colorful galls, as numerous as Christmas decorations on some trees. The massive crop of acorns produced in some years makes for slippery walking underneath.

Both the European and the American Sycamores turn tan. Many of them start turning in mid-summer as they fight against anthracnose, a fungal disease. The sycamore seed balls hang on the trees alone as the leaves fall, and you can watch the birds tearing them apart for a feast on a cold morning.

The pecans and walnuts also turn brown, with a few red highlights in the pecans and yellow tones in the walnuts. I enjoy watching the crows picking up the nuts and dropping them repeatedly until they crack open.

Persimmons grow naturally in the Southeast United States and in southern Asia. They are well acclimated in Visalia. Most of the trees here are grafted to produce Asian type persimmons, either

Chinese Elm

A greener, milder yellow can be found in most ash trees. Mulberries, if not clipped before they can show their beauty, turn slowly from bright green to lemon yellow, mixing the two colors on each branch.

The Chinese Elms are covered with small samaras, or winged seed pods, clustered at the base of bright orange yellow leaves. Samaras of maples and

the ones that are very astringent until they are soft (Hachiya), or the ones you can eat like an apple (Fuyu). After their leaves fall, the large sweet fruits hang on the bare branches while the birds and lucky humans feast.

Persimmon

Birds

Visalia is a tree city, and trees attract birds. The Audubon Society's annual bird count takes place in late December. This is part of the largest scientific effort by citizens in the world – Audubon societies all over the western hemisphere, using volunteer amateur and professional birdwatchers, count the numbers and species of birds in 100 places in California, more than 2,000 worldwide. Three counts occur in Tulare County – Springville (meets at Lake Success), Sequoia (in and around Sequoia National Park) and Kaweah (around Kaweah Oaks Preserve).

There are many bird species that live here year round and many more that travel through on their way south or north. If we start with the obvious, American Crows are very common, usually in groups of three or more. Also some smaller black birds may still be here – the glossy ones with yellow eyes are male Brewer's Blackbirds (females are an inconspicuous brown).

Northern Mockingbird
(Photo by Gary Lindquist)

Mockingbirds are less visible this time of year. Many move farther south for the winter. They do not sing and defend territory as much in the winter as they do during mating season, when I have seen them chasing crows and even cats away from nesting sites. They often sit out on wires or on the highest branch of a tree where they can easily be seen in their elegant gray and white plumage. Watch for white outer tail feathers and white wing patches when they fly.

The common jay in Visalia is the Western Scrub Jay – it is a paler blue and does not have a crest like the officially named Blue Jay that occurs east of the Rocky Mountains. Jays are related to crows and act like them.

Western Scrub Jay
(Photo by Gary Lindquist)

The gulls that appear all over parks and school fields in December are Ring-billed Gulls. Many winter here and spend summers around lakes east of the Sierras. Some fields attract flocks of cattle egrets – beautiful white birds that fly off in the late morning to feed in the winter wet agricultural fields during the day. While you are looking at the larger birds on the grassy fields in Visalia, also scan for Killdeer. These small birds with long legs are commonly seen run-

Other conspicuous birds in town are woodpeckers. The two common species here are Northern Flickers and Acorn Woodpeckers. Both fly from tree to tree or pole with a distinctive style that looks as if they are often about to crash. They fold their wings after a few strokes and seem to open them up just before they stall in flight. Acorn Woodpeckers are responsible for drilling holes in telephone poles and inserting acorns all over town.

Cattle Egrets gather on a field in Visalia
(Photo by Gary Lindquist)

Acorn Woodpecker stuffing a prize into a hole
(Photo by Gary Lindquist)

ning around on fields, especially along the edges and in neglected spots where they can forage and – in the spring – lay their eggs in exposed nests right out in the open.

If you have a feeder you will see some smaller birds that are common here. The House Finch is a mostly brown bird with some red coloring on males this time of year. In the spring the male finch's chest and head turn bright red. White-crowned Sparrows also like the free handouts. These active small birds look like they are wearing a fancy football helmet with three white stripes

House Finch
(Photo by Gary Lindquist)

Lesser Goldfinch
(Photo by Gary Lindquist)

on it. House Sparrows – imported from Europe – also abound. The males are easily recognized by their black bibs. If you are lucky, an Anna's Hummingbird may still be around. Keep fresh sugar water out – sometimes an Orange-crowned Warbler will try out the hummingbird feeder, too.

Cedar Waxwing
(Photo by Gary Lindquist)

Other small birds hide in the trees and bushes. Stand still and look carefully into your yard thickets. A flock of Cedar Waxwings may be there. You could find a bright Goldfinch pulling seeds out

Anna's Hummingbird
(Photo by Gary Lindquist)

Western Screech Owl
(Photo by Gary Lindquist)

Mountains

While looking at the trees and the birds, do not forget to also look at the mountains, which are clearly visible on many fall and winter days. In a good year with early precipitation, the high peaks are white against the deep blue sky.

Due east of Visalia is Dennison Mountain, which is on the southern edge of Sequoia National Park. The saddle just to the north is where the south fork of the Kaweah River comes out of the high mountains.

Scanning north, you can see the high peaks on the Great Western Divide. The most conspicuous of these is Sawtooth, which takes a bite out of the northern sky. Left of that, the bare, crumbling columns of Castle Rocks may be the remains of a building smashed by a rock catapulted from Sawtooth. On a really clear day you can see the gray mass of Moro Rock below, with Alta Peak looming above it. Over half of Tulare County is in the mountains. Make a plan for this month's walk to include some snowshoeing or skiing in Sequoia National Park.

of Liquidambar balls. A Sharp-shinned Hawk or even a Screech Owl may be hiding in the branches of any large tree. An Anna's Hummingbird could be sitting on a branch before darting to the next flower.

If you looked very carefully all over Visalia you could find more than 200 species of birds, from ducks to owls, sandpipers to hummingbirds to hawks. Join a Tulare County Audubon Society field trip to learn from the experts.

The Sierras in December. Castle Rocks is on the far left

The trunk of the Paradise Oak is 15 feet, 8 inches in circumference.

Valley Oaks

The City of Visalia officially protects Valley Oaks with a strong and enforced ordinance, which states:

The citizens of Visalia are fortunate to live among the largest remaining stand of native Valley Oaks in the Central Valley. These magnificent trees need to be protected during development, so they will survive for the next generation. The City's Valley Oak Ordinance establishes policies for the care, trimming and removal of Valley Oaks. Residents and developers are required to ensure the protection of these magnificent trees and must obtain permission to remove or prune Valley Oaks.

When a Valley Oak must be removed, a mitigation fee is imposed and the money is saved in the Oak Tree Maintenance Fund, which is used to plant Valley Oaks in public areas and helps low-income residents maintain their trees. There are standards for building near Valley Oak trees, and developers must submit a "Valley Oak Tree Management Plan" before beginning a project.

Oak Growth

The California White Oak or Valley Oak (*Quercus lobata*) commonly grows to more than fifteen feet in circumference, with the largest specimen recorded a massive 28 feet in circumference. The largest Valley Oak living today is in Tulare County (in the yard of a home between Tulare and Visalia) and has a circumference over 23 feet.

The Valley Oak leaf canopy is wide and full. The branches start growing up at an angle, but as they lengthen they become pendant; some twigs reach to the ground from mid-tree height. Each branch twists and turns, with barely a foot of straight wood before the next branchlet.

The leaves appear in March, starting out a light, bright green, but soon they take on a solid mid-green shade with a dusty tint. The leaves vary from tiny – 1 inch long – to 7 inches or more. They can be deeply lobed and sharp-toothed or rounded and soft, all on the same tree. Often larger leaves are near the trunk, where they grow bigger to photosynthesize better in the shade.

Inconspicuous flowers appear in March and April about the same time that the leaves come out. Some oaks flower and leaf out earlier than others,

Two leaves from the same Valley Oak tree

Valley Oak flowers

This eight-year-old oak is slowly straightening its trunk.

but by mid-April all oaks should be in new leaf. The pollen is an allergen to some people. Acorns start forming in May and continue to grow until the weather cools. Then the caps dry and they fall. The leaves drop in mid-December.

The trunk is sturdy but often bent – small trees are likely to lean to one side or the other, making up for the slant by growing more branches on the other side. Most will straighten as they age by putting wider growth rings where needed until the trunk is upright. The bark on mature trees is dark gray-brown, with deep v-shaped furrows making patterns. Scars and burls add character with interesting growth patterns that show on the outer bark.

Acorns

The long, sharp-pointed acorns fall copiously in many years, less so in others. The California Ground Squirrel collects them as do pack rats (Mexican Wood Rats and other species). Early settlers watched grizzly bears gather in the late fall and camp under the trees feasting. They pulled down branches to get at the acorns and even sent the cubs up into the trees to break off acorn-laden branches and throw them down.

Northern Flickers and Acorn Woodpeckers also collect these seeds. They "plant" them in utility poles and other dead wood. Crows and jays sometimes pick them up and drop them on the street to crack them, but these birds much prefer the walnuts, pecans, and almonds that grow wild all over Visalia.

Acorns were a staple food for the Yokuts Indians who lived here, but they preferred the Black Oak acorns which they gathered as they made their way down from their summer camps in the foothills. Black Oaks occur above 2500 ft. altitude and do not grow well on the valley floor.

The first white people to record a trip near Visalia probably came near to what is now Mooney Grove Park in about 1806. These were Spanish explorers from the coastal missions, who were looking for stolen horses as well as a possible place to establish an interior mission. They never did set up a mission – it was far too difficult to get here through the swamplands around Tulare Lake. Communication and supplies would be almost impossible. Plus the natives were not very hospitable; they had probably heard about what was going on along the coast and wanted no part of it. But the Spaniards were impressed with the dry areas above Tulare Lake and the majestic oaks that gave them needed shade.

When settlers arrived in this valley, many areas were park-like, with large oaks all about and native grasses growing underneath in their protection. Early settlers found the oaks in their way and cleared many of them to make way for farms, while they realized the value of the trees for shade and always kept some around their homes. By the early 1900s the loss of oaks was being noted, as in this article from the Bakersfield Morning Echo newspaper in 1904.

It is a very sad fact to record that those fine groves of handsome oak trees that nature planted about the country between Tulare and Visalia are being rapidly wiped out by the wood-chopper's ax. Many of the finest of them have already been reduced to a dreary stretch of stumpage and others are dotted with the white tents of the destroyers. Since the first settlers came to Tulare County, these oak trees have been its chief feature of beauty and attractiveness. They have tempered the weeds in winter and summer. They have been a godsend to the picnicker and the wayfarer and have given the country a picturesque, woodsy and home like appearance in sharp contrast to desert plains both to the north and south. (Quoted by Terry Ommen in *Historic Happenings Newsletter* April 2010.)

The wood is fair for firewood, although it burns quickly and leaves lots of ashes.

It makes terrible lumber – it's difficult to find a wood that twists and splits more than the Valley Oak wood does as it dries. Fort Visalia was built with Valley Oak logs, cut over ten feet long and split in half. These timbers were "planted" in a 3 foot deep ditch, with earth tamped around them. Digging the holes would not have been hard; the land here is all a floodplain, but the chore of chopping the oaks down and splitting them seems nearly impossible. Lifting large logs up into the ditch must have taken lots of ingenuity as well as muscle power – Valley Oak logs are heavy! In a year or two, the fort would have had a distinct snaggle-toothed look as the oak logs twisted and bent as they dried.

Oak Galls

In the late summer various small wasps use the oaks for breeding grounds – their activities cause galls to form on twigs or on leaves. These galls protect the insects' eggs, which change into larvae and then emerge in the spring as adults. The most conspicuous of these is the "Oak Apple" gall which grows large and round on twigs. It is made by the Oak Gall Wasp,

Left: Galls made by the wasp *Andricus Kingii*
Right: Galls made by the wasp *Antron Douglassii*

Andricus quercuscalifornicus. The galls do not harm trees and fall off when no longer needed.

Nut to Tree

Acorns sprout easily. If they fall in a protected place the trees will start growing when the weather warms and be up to 15 inches tall by autumn. A taproot pushes down as fast as the sprout grows on top, but it starts putting out rootlets quickly while the little trunk is usually straight with one or no branches. This taproot will continue to grow for the first year or more of the tree's life, but then it gives way to spreading roots that grow out from the bole of the tree to gather nutrients and moisture. After a few years

A seedling starts.

Two- and three-year-old trees along Mill Creek.

Twig galls made by the Oak Gall Wasp, *Andricus quercuscalifornicus*

the little oak is a real tree. In fifteen years it may be three feet in circumference and over 15 feet high. An oak at the corner of Grant and Feemster in Visalia was a volunteer sprout in 1980. In 2010 it was 6 feet 6 inches in circumference. The Evers Oak in the Visalia Cemetery was planted as an acorn in 1911 and is now 10 feet 5 inches in circumference.

Valley Oaks can live more than 300 years. Superannuated trees start to drop limbs and may be partially hollow. They become shorter and more twisted with the ravages of time, shrinking into themselves as they slowly return to the earth. Hollow cavities rot and expand until the tree falls.

Mature oaks in a Visalia field are between 75 and 150 years old.

The oldest Valley Oak in Visalia was cut down in September 2010.

Bibliography

Allen, William. *It Started in the Stable*. (Private Printing), 2011. The history of St. Mary's Church and the George McCann Catholic School.

Los Tulares – Tulare County Historical Society newsletter. Published 4 times per year.

Mayfield, Thomas Jefferson. *Indian Summer: Traditional Life among the Choinumni Indians of California's San Joaquin Valley*. Heyday Books, 1993. First published in 1923, this remarkable account is the living testimony of a man who was left by his father to be raised by the local Indians near Terra Bella.

Mitchell, Annie. *The Way It Was: The Colorful History of Tulare County*. Valley Publishers, Fresno, 1976. This excellent work compiles Annie Mitchell's years of research on the history of this area.

Ommen, Terry. *Historic Happenings Newsletter*. www.visaliahistory.blogspot.com. This blog is an entertaining and informative way to keep up with Visalia's history.

Ommen, Terry. *Visalia, Then and Now*. Arcadia Publishing, 2008. This fun book has pictures of well-known Visalia buildings coupled with historic pictures of the same spots. Ommen's interesting commentaries bring out the history.

Pavlik, Bruce M. [et.al.] *Oaks of California*. Cachuma Press, 1991. Excellent descriptions of the many Oak species in California are enhanced by historical quotes and stories, plus superb photographs.

Pilling, George. *History of Tulare County* (web site) www.tularecountyhistory.org. This web site is intended for third grade students studying Tulare County history. It is open to anyone to contribute.

San Joaquin Valley & Sierra Foothills Photo Heritage (web site) http://sjvls.org/photoheritage/index.html. This web site of pictures is constantly being expanded.

Visalia's Heritage: Buildings, People, History. Visalia Heritage Incorporated. 1986. Pictures and short histories of many houses and businesses in Visalia.

Visalia: A Pictorial History 1850s–1950s. Visalia Heritage Incorporated. 2002. A collection of pictures of events, people, and buildings in Visalia.

Index